CLEP

American Literature
Exam

SECRETS

Study Guide
Your Key to Exam Success

CLEP Test Review for the
College Level Examination Program

Dear Future Exam Success Story:

Congratulations on your purchase of our study guide. Our goal in writing our study guide was to cover the content on the test, as well as provide insight into typical test taking mistakes and how to overcome them.

Standardized tests are a key component of being successful, which only increases the importance of doing well in the high-pressure high-stakes environment of test day. How well you do on this test will have a significant impact on your future, and we have the research and practical advice to help you execute on test day.

The product you're reading now is designed to exploit weaknesses in the test itself, and help you avoid the most common errors test takers frequently make.

How to use this study guide

We don't want to waste your time. Our study guide is fast-paced and fluff-free. We suggest going through it a number of times, as repetition is an important part of learning new information and concepts.

First, read through the study guide completely to get a feel for the content and organization. Read the general success strategies first, and then proceed to the content sections. Each tip has been carefully selected for its effectiveness.

Second, read through the study guide again, and take notes in the margins and highlight those sections where you may have a particular weakness.

Finally, bring the manual with you on test day and study it before the exam begins.

Your success is our success

We would be delighted to hear about your success. Send us an email and tell us your story. Thanks for your business and we wish you continued success.

Sincerely,

Mometrix Test Preparation Team

Need more help? Check out our flashcards at:
http://MometrixFlashcards.com/CLEP

TABLE OF CONTENTS

Top 20 Test Taking Tips

1. Carefully follow all the test registration procedures
2. Know the test directions, duration, topics, question types, how many questions
3. Setup a flexible study schedule at least 3-4 weeks before test day
4. Study during the time of day you are most alert, relaxed, and stress free
5. Maximize your learning style; visual learner use visual study aids, auditory learner use auditory study aids
6. Focus on your weakest knowledge base
7. Find a study partner to review with and help clarify questions
8. Practice, practice, practice
9. Get a good night's sleep; don't try to cram the night before the test
10. Eat a well balanced meal
11. Know the exact physical location of the testing site; drive the route to the site prior to test day
12. Bring a set of ear plugs; the testing center could be noisy
13. Wear comfortable, loose fitting, layered clothing to the testing center; prepare for it to be either cold or hot during the test
14. Bring at least 2 current forms of ID to the testing center
15. Arrive to the test early; be prepared to wait and be patient
16. Eliminate the obviously wrong answer choices, then guess the first remaining choice
17. Pace yourself; don't rush, but keep working and move on if you get stuck
18. Maintain a positive attitude even if the test is going poorly
19. Keep your first answer unless you are positive it is wrong
20. Check your work, don't make a careless mistake

American Literature

Colonial Period (1620–1830)

Of Plymouth Plantation

Faith is the central theme found in Bradford's *Of Plymouth Plantation*. The Puritans looked solely to God for guidance in overcoming numerous obstacles, and accepted the outcome as his divine will. An example of this is when they encountered fierce storms at sea, and committed themselves to the will of God, deciding to proceed. Upon reaching land in safety, they fell to their knees and praised God for delivering them from danger. They believed he spared their lives because they selflessly cared for the ill. The sailors, however, who did not care for the ill, became very ill themselves and died. The Puritans believed God did not spare their lives because of their selfishness. *Of Plymouth Plantation* depicts the beliefs upon which American values, ideologies, and government were established.

Sinners in the Hands of an Angry God

Using strong verbiage and imagery, Jonathan Edwards's "Sinners in the Hands of an Angry God" is meant to remind his congregation that the consequences of sin are severe to the point of horrific. The terrors and punishment that await sinners are depicted in graphic detail, while imagery of a fiery hell is meant to fill the congregation's hearts with fear. And though he wanted them to understand the reality of hell, the sermon was also meant to remind them that through genuine repentance, and seeking the "mere pleasure of God," there is a light at the end of the tunnel. Edwards wanted his congregation to fully understand that the inherited depravity of humanity was not cured through church membership, but personal salvation.

Letters from an American Farmer

American society and all of its manifestations provide the introduction to de Crevecoeur's *Letters from an American Farmer*, attempting to answer the question posed in his first letter, "What is an American?" With vivid descriptions of America's landscape, institutions and people, De Crevecoeur creates a universal American identity, not one divided by various colonies. He celebrates the culture's innocence, simplicity, religious tolerance, and diversity, while exploring the concept of the American dream. From the whaling communities of Martha's Vineyard to southern plantation culture, de Crevecoeur depicts a melting pot of individuals who were "once scattered all over Europe" but in America have "incorporated into one of the finest systems of population which has ever appeared."

The Journal of John Woolman

John Woolman believed strongly in love and protectiveness of all living things, and was deeply distressed by the concept of slavery, finding it to be contradictory to Christianity. In Woolman's company, a fellow Quaker, or "Friend" as they were called, spoke in support of slave trade, believing that Negroes were the offspring of Cain. His justification was "that it was the design of providence they should be slaves, as a condition proper to the race of so wicked a man as Cain was." Another Friend agreed, and Woolman replied that only Noah and his family survived the flood, therefore the bloodline of Cain was destroyed, leaving no descendents. Woolman was immensely troubled by the "darkness of their imaginations." He expressed his belief that all human beings have a right to liberty, and their arguments were merely meant to justify man's "love of ease and gain."

The Way to Wealth: Preface to Poor Richard

Always be employed in something useful is Franklin's primary message in "The Way to Wealth: Preface to Poor Richard." In this context, the virtue of "industry" is defined as hard work. Franklin strongly believed that God helps those who help themselves. While industry leads to making a man "healthy, wealthy and wise," laziness leads only to poverty. Franklin believed that far worse than heavy taxes laid on by the government are the taxes we incur by idleness, pride and folly. Do not put off until tomorrow what you can do today was Franklin's philosophy, and that all time, including leisure time, is meant for doing something useful. In Franklin's words, "God gives all things to Industry."

The American Crisis

In Thomas Paine's *The American Crisis*, he is strongly persuading the colonists, who needed a great deal of inspiration, to fight for freedom. The writings were meant to bolster the morale of the men, and clarify how much was at stake if they failed to fight. He effectively employs analogy in his writings by comparing the king to a thief who breaks into his home, threatens his life, sets fire to his belongings, and demands that only his will be done. By asking the question "Am I to suffer it?" he is urging the colonists to stand up and fight, not sit back and take it. By personalizing the situation in such a way, he persuades them to understand that the power to enslave a people can belong only to God, not to a king.

First Inaugural Address

In his *First Inaugural Address*, Thomas Jefferson sought to reach out to his political opponents, and to mend the breach between Federalists and Republicans. He addresses the opposition, stating now that the voice of the nation has been heard, it is time to "unite in common efforts for the common good." To unify the people, he appeals to them as Americans by stating, "We are all republicans, we are all federalists," reminding them that America is a nation in which even error of opinion is to be tolerated, and where "reason is left free to combat it." "Equal and exact justice" to all men of "whatever state or persuasion" is also a primary component of his message, recognizing equal treatment of all in regard to freedom and justice.

A Model of Christian Charity

In *A Model of Christian Charity*, Winthrop reflects on the extent to which a wealthy citizen has a duty to assist others, both inside and outside the community. He ponders whether the wealthy are obligated to serve the poor, even if it means not being repaid, and even if it means becoming poor themselves. He also states that wealth can create distance between man and God, as excess leads people toward the sins of pride and disregard for others' social needs. However, he does not believe wealth is a bad thing. Wealth, after all, can reflect the glory of God, can be used for the good of the religious state, and should be used for one's own family. But ultimately, Winthrop contends that the wealthy have a Christian responsibility to help others, and "stand aside till his turn be served."

The Journal of Madam Knight

Sarah Kemble Knight, often referred to as "Madam Knight" by her students, kept a diary that told of her experiences when traveling from Boston to New York. Published posthumously, this diary became known as *The Journal of Madam Knight*, in which she was the central character. She took the journey on horseback, something that was unheard of for a woman in this day, and with much humor, tells of the discomforts she encountered. When arriving at one destination she says, "But our Hostes, being a pretty full mouth'd old creature, entertain'd our fellow travailer, the French Doctor, with Innumerable complaints of her bodily infirmities; and whispered to him so lou'd, that all the House had as full a hearing as hee; which was very diverting to the company, (of which there was a great many,) as one might see by their sneering."

Ebenezer Cooke's "The Sotweed Factor"

The "hero" in Ebenezer Cooke's "The Sotweed Factor" comes to America in pursuit of a better life, only to instead encounter bad manners, theft, outlandish food and eating habits, intellectual poverty, lack of education, and a con-artist who defrauds him of all his wealth and property. Even the lawyer he hires turns out to be an "ambodexter quack" who confuses the two professions in which he claims to work. "The Sotweed Factor" is a satirical poem written to satirize the laws, courts, government and constitutions of the country, as well as the entertainments, buildings, and drunkenness of those who inhabited that part of America. However, it is a two-sided satire thesis, or "double-edged satire," also satirizing the speaker himself, who demonstrates foolishness and naiveté when compared to the seasoned colonials.

A Narrative of the Captivity and Restoration of Mrs. Mary Rowlandson

A Narrative of the Captivity and Restoration of Mrs. Mary Rowlandson, by Mary Rowlandson, is a captivity narrative, a genre that stemmed from the violent clash between Indians and Massachusetts's British colonists during King Phillip's war. Rowlandson and her three children, Joseph, Mary and Sarah, were taken as hostages by the Indians for nearly twelve weeks. She recounts how, despite witnessing the death of friends and her youngest daughter, Sarah, and suffering starvation and depression, she relied on her faith in God's providence to sustain her during her suffering and captivity. This reinforced the concept of providence as preached 40 years earlier by the founding Puritans. She viewed this trial as a test of faith, and finally she was reunited with her husband. This book became one of the era's best sellers and provided a great deal of insight into the relationship between the Indians and Puritan colonists.

Poems and Prose

The Prologue

I am obnoxious to each carping tongue, Who says my hand a needle better fits; A poet's pen all scorn I should thus wrong, For such despite they cast on female wits, If what I do prove well, it won't advance; They'll say it's stol'n, or else it was by chance

The excerpt from Anne Bradstreet's "The Prologue" is suggesting that, as a woman, her place is in the home only, and perhaps her hand is better suited for sewing than writing. She further states that if she does happen to compose something that is quite good, she will not get credit for it, as men will claim her work was by chance, or perhaps even stolen from someone else. Bradstreet is expressing her frustration with the prevalent attitude in Puritan society that a woman who dared to express intelligence or a desire to accomplish something outside of the home was unfeminine, and even unacceptable. Through tongue-and-cheek expression, she acknowledges that she understands her role in Puritan society, but does not agree with it.

Upon a Spider Catching a Fly

In Edward Taylor's "Upon a Spider Catching a Fly," the spider represents Satan, and the wasp and the fly two types of sinners caught in his "web." In this "dance of death," the fly is weak and becomes the spider's prey with little to no effort. The wasp, on the other hand, may get caught in Satan's web, but manages to find the strength to escape. The weak fly represents the unsaved. Satan easily devours it because it is unarmed. And while the wasp is still vulnerable to getting caught in the web, it has the strength of salvation to escape, despite Satan's soothing and seductive ways. Taylor warns that we are all sinners, and to be aware of Satan's entrapments, as they can be aimed at us either directly or indirectly. As we see with the wasp, it is only through salvation that we have any hope of escaping this danger.

The Indian Burying Ground

In spite of all l the learned have said, I still my old opinion keep, The posture, that we give the dead, Points out the soul's eternal sleep.
Not so the ancients of these lands—The Indian, when from life released, Again is seated with his friends, And shares again the joyous feast.

Philip Freneau is describing the way Indian tribes buried their dead in a sitting posture, as opposed to the white man's tradition of placing the dead in the posture of "sleep." In the first passage, he is stating that the lying down posture indicates western culture's belief in the eternal sleep of the soul, thus death is an event of great sadness in which mourning is the tradition. This is in direct contrast to the way of the Native Americans, who despite death of the physical body, still remain among their natural surroundings in upright celebration. "Joyous feast" indicates that this is a happy event, again, directly contrasting the depiction of the dead who are laid to rest in a sleeping position. The Indians' belief that the soul lives eternally is cause for celebration, and it is reflected in their positioning of the deceased.

Contemplations

1. When I behold the heavens as in their prime, And then the earth, though old, still clad in green, The stones and trees insensible of time, Nor age nor wrinkle on their front are seen; If winter come, and greenness then do fade, A spring returns, and they more youthful made. But man grows old, lies down, remains where once he's laid.

2. Shall I then praise the heavens, the trees, the earth, Because their beauty and their strength last longer? Shall I wish there or never to had birth, Because they're bigger and their bodies stronger? Nay, they shall darken, perish, fade, and die, And when unmade so ever shall they lie, but man was made for endless immortality.

In the first passage from Anne Bradstreet's "Contemplations," she provides imagery of a green earth, personifies stones and trees as showing no age and having no wrinkle. And although winter comes and the earth is no longer green, youth is restored when spring comes again. She is saying that though the seasons come, vibrant, then faded, then vibrant once again, man simply grows old and dies, never to be renewed again as nature is through the seasons. However in the second passage, she is stating that nature will someday surely die a physical death, though it is stronger than the human body. But unlike the stones and the trees of nature, man has an immortal soul, and therefore lives forever.

The War Inevitable

They tell us, Sir, that we are weak—unable to cope with so formidable an adversary. But when shall we be stronger? Will it be the next week or the next year? Will it be when we are totally disarmed and when a British guard shall be stationed in every house?

Three millions of People, armed in the holy cause of liberty, and in such a country as that which we possess, are invincible by any force which our enemy can send against us.

Gentlemen may cry, Peace, Peace!—but there is no peace. The war is actually begun!

In the first passage, Patrick Henry is responding to an accusation of weakness through the use of rhetorical questions. In the second passage, he appeals to the cause and the vastness of the American army, instilling confidence that America can withstand the enemy's attack. He then reminds them of the futility of holding out for peace when, in actuality, war has already been declared upon them. Well-organized, articulate points provide support for Henry's argument, while the use of simile, personification, and rhetorical questions help him appeal to his listeners on an even deeper emotional level. Though the literary elements are apparent in written form, Henry was one of the great orators, who brought his prose to life in spoken form.

Historical and Social Settings

The Day of Doom

With its apocalyptic theme, this collection of poems addresses both salvation and judgment. Addressing the readers with vivid imagery of "doom," repentance and prayers, Michael Wigglesworth depicts the horrors that await the unrepentant sinner, including infants and children. Though harsh by today's standards, punishment of sin, fear of God and hope only through salvation were common themes of Puritan writings. Its popularity among the Puritans can be measured by its readership, as it was the most widely read book in colonial America and continued to be published through numerous editions for more than a century.

Phillis Wheatley

Phillis Wheatley has been called America's first important black writer, and she was, in fact, the first African American to publish a book and earn a living from her writing. Born in Gambia, Africa, she was sold into slavery at age seven, and brought to Boston, Massachusetts on a ship called "Phillis," which she took as her name. She initially worked as an attendant for the wife of a tailor and merchant, who taught her how to read and write English. She adopted the Christian faith, was raised with the family's other children, and, at age 13, wrote her first poem. Though she rarely discusses her situation in her works, she does so in the poem, "On Being Brought from Africa to America," in which she reveals deep gratitude for her Christianity and new life in America.

William Bartram

John Bartram, father of William Bartram, was a man of science who established the first botanical garden in the United States near Philadelphia. It was on these grounds that William was raised, thus forming his lifelong love of nature. As an adult, he traveled widely, particularly throughout the southeast, the inspiration for his famous *Travels through North and South Carolina, Georgia, East and West Florida*. Throughout *Travels*, imagery abounds, from the rich description of plants, to animals in their natural habitat. Roaring alligators, thousands of fish, tropical blossoms and over 200 species of birds are depicted in a writing style that directly influenced famous poets of the time, such as Shelley and Wordsworth. For the next century, his work would continue to influence American and foreign writers.

Literary Devices

An important characteristic of Colonial American literature is that writing should have a practical purpose. Discuss at least two common forms of writing during this period, cite one example of each, and explain how the writing demonstrates a practical purpose.

Two common forms of writing in Colonial American literature were diaries and sermons. *The Diary of Samuel Sewall* was of traditional Puritan style, and reflects his desire for living well. Clear, vivid, and filled with insight into Sewall's spiritual and earthly concerns, this piece actually served two practical purposes:
- it provided an outlet for Sewall to understand and work through his difficulties and uncertainties and
- it still today remains an excellent reference tool for understanding Colonial times

Cotton Mather published approximately 450 books and pamphlets based on his sermons, which were probably the most common form of writing during this period. In his sermon "The Duties of Children to their Parents," Mather addresses the fifth commandment, compares the authority of mothers to that of fathers, and describes the fate met by "undutiful" children. The purpose of this, as with all of his sermons, was to educate people of all ages on what is expected of us by God, a common theme written in a common form by the Puritans.

Romantic Period (1830–1870)

Rip Van Winkle

Washington Irving's "Rip Van Winkle" is set in a small Dutch village of the Catskill Mountains near the Hudson River. Rip Van Winkle is a fun-loving but lazy man, and his house is a mess, for which he is constantly nagged by his wife. To escape his wife's nagging, one day Rip and his dog Wolf go into the hills, where they encounter a man carrying a heavy keg. He assists the man with the keg, carrying it to an open field where small, bearded men were bowling—a sound he previously mistakes for thunder. Rip drinks three glasses of the tasty drink and falls asleep in the moonlight. He awakes to what he thinks is the next day, but, wandering into town, discovers it is 20 years later. His wife has died, and he has missed the entire American Revolution. Some believe his story, and some think he is crazy. Rip then lives a happy existence with his daughter and her family. Occasionally, he hears the sound of thunder in the mountains, but he never returns, so as not to lose another 20 years.

The Last of the Mohicans

Set during the French and Indian War, James Fenimore Cooper's *The Last of the Mohicans* chronicles the massacre of the colonial garrison at Fort William Henry, and tells of a fictional kidnapping of two pioneer sisters by Magua, who is seeking revenge. When the character Hawkeye identifies Magua as a possible traitor, the plot then revolves around the clash of these characters and the chase that follows. The story is filled with action, suspense and adventure. Cooper's depiction of the natives, particularly the Uncas and Chingachgook, were romanticized and sympathetic, for which he drew much criticism. Many believed the portrayal was idealized and unrealistic, and that Magua was portrayed as being far too villainous. However, *The Last of the Mohicans* was loved by readers and was Cooper's most successful and popular work.

Snow-Bound

In "Snow-Bound," by John Greenleaf Whittier, the inmates the author is referring to were his father, mother, brother, two sisters, uncle and aunt, as well as the district schoolmaster who boarded with the family. Filled with beautiful imagery, "Snow-Bound" is a reflection of a boy's tender memories in his family home on a cold, snowy December day. As the snow thickens into the night, the "inmates" of this farmhouse gather around an open fire. He describes each family member one by one through the eyes of a boy, and the stories they told that revealed their interests. The rest of the poem is told through the eyes of someone no longer a boy, depicting cherished memories engraved infinitely on the human heart.

Uncle Tom's Cabin

Characters in Harriet Beecher Stowe's *Uncle Tom's Cabin*
- Uncle Tom
- Eva
- Simon Legree

Uncle Tom, the title character in Harriet Beecher Stowe's *Uncle Tom's Cabin*, is the hero of the story, a noble, long-suffering Christian slave who stands up for his beliefs and is grudgingly admired by even his enemies. Eva is a child who enters the narrative when Uncle Tom is traveling via steamship to New Orleans to be sold. She is rescued by Uncle Tom, who saves her from drowning. She begs her father to buy Tom and he becomes the coachman at the family's plantation. Eva is kind-hearted and talks constantly about love and forgiveness, but eventually falls terminally ill. Simon Legree, a Northerner by birth, is a cruel slave owner who tries to demoralize Tom and break him of his religious faith. Eventually he beats Tom to death out of frustration with Tom's unbreakable belief in God.

Life of Frederick Douglass

Frederick Douglass endures difficulties from the beginning of his early childhood. He recalls only having met his mother a few times. The identity of his father was never certain, but he was possibly Douglass's master, Captain Anthony, a white man. At a young age, Douglass witnessed Captain Anthony beating his aunt until she was bloodied, and he recalls being cold and hungry much of the time. At age 7 or 8, he was sent to live with Mr. and Mrs. Hugh Auld in Baltimore. Mrs. Auld attempted to teach him how to read but was rebuked by her husband. He watched slavery turn her from a kind person into a bitter slaveholder. His darkest time, however, was when he was sent to live with Edward Covey, where he was constantly beaten and overworked. Later at a shipyard, he was beaten by some of the white workers, but eventually learned to calk, and settled in New Bedford, Massachusetts as a free man. He became one of the most influential speakers against slavery in American history.

The Scarlet Letter

Nathaniel Hawthorne's *The Scarlet Letter* is about a beautiful young woman, Hester Prynne, who has an adulterous encounter and bears a child while her husband, Roger Chillingworth, is away in Europe. The setting takes place in Puritan Boston, and her partner in adultery is a highly respected clergyman, Reverend Arthur Dimmesdale, whose identity Hester does not reveal. The plot centers around the public condemnation and scorn endured by Hester, who is made to wear a scarlet-colored letter "A," identifying her as an adulteress. It also focuses on the vengeful reaction of her husband. At first Reverend Dimmesdale lacks the courage to identify himself as the father of Hester's child, but guilt eventually destroys his resistance, and he reveals his identity at the end. *The Scarlet Letter* is about not only the sin of

Hester, but also the reaction to it, focusing on the rigid moral outlook of the Puritans. Though forced to publicly expose her shame with the scarlet letter, Hester acknowledges her sin, lives a respectable life, and eventually earns the respect of the townspeople.

A Fable for Critics

In "A Fable for Critics," James Russell Lowell provides satirical, critical appraisals of American literary figures. Although sometimes exhibiting careless verse, its witty and engaging "brisk Yankee" dialect has allowed it to endure through ever-changing styles in literature. Authors that are satirized in this poem include Ralph Waldo Emerson, Nathaniel Hawthorne and Edgar Allan Poe. Of Emerson, he states that he talks of life, nature, love and God as if they were dead, and though precise and scientific, his works have a sense of being "post mortem." Of Hawthorne, he proclaims his genius, and his wholeness so "perfectly man" that Nature shaped him not with clay but "finer grained" stuff. And of Edgar Allan Poe, he writes, "Three-fifths of him genius and two-fifths sheer fudge," and claims the heart in his writing has somehow been "all squeezed out" by the mind.

The Adventures of Huckleberry Finn

Huck Finn, who lives with his widowed aunt, escapes when his cruel father kidnaps him for financial gain. He sails off on a raft with a slave named Jim, whom he refuses to turn in. Based on your knowledge of the entire story and the above brief synopsis, discuss three themes within *The Adventures of Huckleberry Finn*.

Both Huck and Jim escape a form of oppression. Huck escapes an abusive father and an aunt who makes him feel oppressed due to her constant efforts to "civilize" him, and Jim, who is about to be sold, escapes the oppression of slavery; hence, the first theme is freedom, equality and independence of all human beings. The love of money as the root of all evil is the second theme. Huck's love of money results in his attempted kidnapping by his father, and his father's love of money replaces an ability to love others. It is also is the love of money that allows slavery to thrive. And third, Huck knows the law requires him to turn in his friend Jim, but his moral instincts tell him it is the right thing not to, even though he feels guilty for breaking the law. Thus, the third theme is that moral law supersedes government law.

The Maypole of Merry Mount

In Nathaniel Hawthorne's "The Maypole of Merry Mount," Edith and Edgar, the young couple who marry in a ceremony at the maypole, demonstrate that love and only love can bring people together, make them stay together, and bring them happiness. Immediately after the marriage ceremony, they encounter a test when Endicott threatens them. But instead of cowering, they stand together firmly bound in their love and express a willingness to die for each other. These characters also demonstrate a message of hope. Moved by their devotion to one another, Endicott comes to admire Edgar and Edith, and takes them with him to live among his fellow Puritans. Hope is born because this couple's love will set a good example for the other Puritans, while also making them less suspicious of outsiders.

Success is Counted Sweetest

In Emily Dickinson's "Success is Counted Sweetest," the central theme is that only those who have failed can truly understand the meaning of success. This is depicted in the first stanza of the poem, "Success is counted sweetest by those who ne'er succeed. To comprehend a nectar, requires sorest seed." Nectar symbolizes any delectable drink, something that is "sweet," but originates from the most sour of seed. Paradox is used to express this theme, as it is the defeated who are best qualified to evaluate the impact of success, and not the victors. This observation could apply to anyone who has ever been defeated—for example, an athlete who hears the cheer of the crowd for his opponent, the politician who loses an election, or the job applicant who is not selected.

Walden

Henry David Thoreau's *Walden* chronicles the two years he spent living in a small cabin in the woods next to Walden Pond in Concord, Massachusetts. Throughout this account, Thoreau considers numerous aspects of the world around Walden, and follows the seasons of the year as a framework to discuss nature, wealth, money, academic study and spirituality. A life of simplicity is a theme throughout the book, as he survived off only what he grew on the land near the cabin. He spends a generous portion of the book describing the beauty of Walden Pond, and chronicles his encounters with various people who come to the pond, most of whom are manual laborers. Thoreau also places great emphasis on truth, which he concludes is only known when human beings explore every part of themselves, not the world.

Sut Lovingood: Yarns spun by a Nat'ral Born Durn'd Fool

George Washington Harris wrote 24 "Lovingood" tales, with all but eight being published. Politically overt and published in southern newspapers, these sketches highlight the dialect and customs of people living in the mountains of eastern Tennessee. Funny, bawdy, and at times violent, the stories emphasize mankind's baseness, and the superiority complex of "city folk," who believe they are better in manners, morals and intellect than the "rurals." In many of the stories, Sut challenges authority, and ridicules impoverished mountain people when they contribute to their own debasement. Sut is a character who has rejected all traditional social institutions and lives to eat, drink and womanize, fully aware and content with his own imperfections.

The Horse-Swap and The Fight

In Augustus Baldwin Longstreet's "The Horse-Swap" and "The Fight," both stories begin with rural Georgians in humorous conflict. However, cruelty and violence eventually outweigh their better natures. In "The Horse-Swap," the character Yellow Blossom challenges a local villager to a horse trade. The bargaining provides entertainment to a growing crowd of onlookers until it is revealed that Yellow Blossom has forced his horse to endure a gaping wound for the sport of the trade. Likewise in "The Fight," two men on friendly terms avoid the town's attempt to cajole them into fighting. Though it begins good-naturedly, when their wives insult each other, the men are prodded into chivalric conflict, engaging in a barbaric street battle that leaves each permanently mangled. In both stories, the narrator is simply a remote onlooker, and he creates a stark contrast between his cultivated perspective and the unsophisticated characters he encounters.

Masque of the Red Death

In the dominion of the main character, Prince Prospero, a deadly plague called the "Red Death" is on the rise, killing its victims within a half-hour of the onset of symptoms. Safe in his tightly secured abbey, which no one may enter or leave, the prince holds a masked ball among seven rooms, each decorated in a specific color. Everyone dresses in "masked" costume, and the party is a huge success. But when an ebony clock strikes midnight, the guests notice a tall, thin unidentified masquerader outfitted as a corpse in a grave. Knowing the "guest" is meant to be outfitted as the Red Death, Prince Prospero becomes angry and chases him with a dagger into the "black room." Prospero falls, and when his guests attempt to retaliate, they find nothing under the costume or the mask, as this guest is the actual Red Death. The theme of the story is, that despite every precaution, no man or woman can escape death forever.

Song of Myself

In Walt Whitman's "Song of Myself," the author asks questions and ponders the meaning of life, which he believed to be a mystery. Surrounded by people who draw distinct lines between right and wrong, Whitman rejects such points of view. Instead, he embraces the beauty of all things, finding God in all things, and admitting that human perceptions fall short of true understanding... therefore, God cannot be fully understood. He maintains that nature provides numerous opportunities for interpretation. When a child asks, "What is the grass?" he admits that he does not know the answer any more than the child does, and follows with a series of "guesses," but never definitive answers. He continues to say "I perceive" but falls short of ever stating, "I know." "Song of Myself" contains three themes: the idea of the self, identifying the self with others, and the poet's relationship with nature and the universe.

Representative Men

In 1845, when the nation was still a young American republic, Ralph Waldo Emerson composed *Representative Men*, a series of seven lectures in which he names six people who embody the principles and aspirations of America. By stressing the value of individual greatness, Emerson creates a connection between the reader and his chosen everyday men: Plato, of whom he says, "Plato is philosophy, and philosophy is Plato"; Emanuel Swedenborg, a "remarkable example of the introverted mind"; Michel de Montaigne, "a vigorous and original thinker"; William Shakespeare, who understood "tradition supplies a better fable than any invention can"; Napoleon Bonaparte, who "expresses the tone of thought and belief" with utmost fidelity; and Johann Wolfgang von Goethe, easily able to "pierce coats of convention." By "representative," Emerson did not mean the man who was merely average, but a genius that stands above all others in his field, offered up as examples to our own nation.

The Legend of Sleepy Hollow

In Washington Irving's "The Legend of Sleepy Hollow," Ichabod Crane is an intellectual who fancies himself an "outdoorsy" type. Tall, thin, and narrow-shouldered, he is able to help out with the "lighter labors" on the farm, but is confined by a build that matches that of the bird that bears his surname. His fiction being more exciting than reality, however, Ichabod chooses to see himself in a different light. Crane delights in telling ghoulish tales about the legend of Sleepy Hollow, a headless horseman who rides every night in search of his head. On the trek home, his own tales frighten him into seeing all sorts of figures in the dark. Despondent one night after being refused by his love interest Katrina, Crane hears a horseman following him, and he then disappears. Is it imagined, or is it real? Although someone claims later that Ichabod Crane is alive, his rival, Brom Bones, bears a knowing look. "The Legend of Sleepy Hollow" serves a lesson in keeping lines clear between fiction and reality.

The House of the Seven Gables

Hepzibah is an old, ill-tempered individual who finds herself forced to open a small cent shop in the face of growing impoverishment.
 Clifford, Hepziba's brother, is a man on the verge of insanity, due to being imprisoned for 30 years for a crime he did not commit.

Judge Jaffrey, a much-respected man of the world, is wealthy, powerful, and held in high regard by his community. He is also thought to be a prospective candidate for governorship.

Phoebe is pretty, optimistic and outgoing; she is the heroine of the novel. A distant relative of the Pyncheon family, she comes to the house from the farm on which she grew up, and her arrival brings about a reversal in the fortunes of the Pyncheon family.

Holgrave is an artist and the old enemy of the Pyncheons, who falls in love with Phoebe.

The Song of Hiawatha

In the section of the poem called "Hiawatha's Childhood," Henry Wadsworth Longfellow recounts the adventures of an Ojibwa or Chippewa chief he named Hiawatha. Raised on the southern shore of Lake Superior by his grandmother, the old Nokomis, Hiawatha has a heart to lead his people in the ways of peace and prosperity, while also possessing the courage and skill to conquer evil. The Indian hero has human traits as well as super powers, and the epic poem incorporates numerous elements that captivate audiences, including magicians, fierce battles, giants, and even a giant sturgeon that swallows Hiawatha whole. "The Song of Hiawatha" became one of the best-known American poems, with the famous lines, "On the shores of Gitche Gumee, Of the shining Big-Sea-Water."

The Big Bear of Arkansas

T. B. Thorpe's "The Big Bear of Arkansas" is a masterpiece of southwestern humor. Thorpe describes a group on a Mississippi steamboat. He then introduces Jim Doggett, and allows Jim to tell of his big contest with the bear. As a man from Arkansas, Jim recognizes a difference between himself and New Orleans men and admits to having difficulty even talking to them. But he tells a story with details more splendid than those actually provided by Arkansas, and works into the story "Shirt-tail Bend," Jim's own place. Half of the story is preparing for the story of the bear hunt itself. When he does tell of the bear, it grows to the size of a "black mist" and becomes a supernatural being. Thorpe makes a return appearance for the story's conclusion, and states that Jim is the first to break the silence following his tale.

The Symphony

In Sidney Lanier's highly regarded poem "The Symphony," Lanier is protesting materialism by denouncing the inhumanity of commercialism and promoting the beneficent forces of love. Lanier, himself a musician with a symphony, structured the poem like the parts of a symphony orchestra. For instance, violins describe how trade has created poverty and oppression. The flutes describe transcendent nature. The clarinets admonish against prostitution. The horns celebrate chivalry. And finally the symphony hears a plea for a return to innocence by the "ancient wise bassoons." As in any symphony, each section has its own unique part, and combines to create a musical masterpiece. Lanier ends the poem and reveals his artistic vision with this reflection: "And yet shall Love himself be heard, Though long deferred, though long deferred: O'er the modern waste a dove hath whirred: Music is Love in search of a word."

The Marshes of Glynn

Considered one of his greatest works, "The Marshes of Glynn" by Sidney Lanier is part of an unfinished set of lyrical nature poems known as the "Hymns of the Marshes." Like all the poems within the set, "The Marshes of Glynn" describes the vast, open salt marshes of Glynn County on the coast of Georgia, and it was inspired by the poet's visit to Brunswick. This "nature poem" celebrates the transcendent spirit within nature, and is in fact a loving tribute to nature and spirituality. The poem begins with a description of the thick marsh, and the narrator feels himself growing and connecting with the sinews of the marsh itself. His vision then expands beyond the marsh and seaward. As he contemplates the vastness of the marshes, he is struck by the mystery and power that they hold, and recognizes them to be an expression of "the greatness of God." Although Lanier intended to write six "Hymns of the Marshes," poor health only allowed him to complete three others: "Sunrise," "Individuality," and "Marsh Song—at Sunset."

Roughing It

Roughing It, by Mark Twain, is a humorous collection of facts as well as a travel journal, depicting his journey from St. Louis to San Francisco, and on to Hawaii in the early 1860s. The backdrop of this adventure-filled novel is the explosion of the mining business in the Western States of the Union, and more specifically, the Territory of Nevada. He traveled west by stagecoach, to serve as his brother Orion's personal secretary, who had secured the position of Secretary of the Nevada Territory. Twain recounts his experiences as a frontier newspaper reporter, prospector and writer, and examines the economic boom of the area and its consequences on the people. He also delves into the evolution of English as a diversified language, and the transformation of nature by man. Throughout the novel, the tone remains primarily humorous, providing a semi-autobiographical account of the author's mistakes and mishaps that prevent him from fulfilling his "get rich with little effort" ambitions.

Passage to India

In 1869, Walt Whitman wrote "Passage to India," celebrating several present achievements of the time: the building and engineering achievement of the Suez Canal, the laying of the Atlantic cable, and the completion of the transcontinental railroad. He attributes these accomplishments to the past, stating, "For what is the present, after all, but a growth out of the past?" Whitman is enthralled by world religions, and praises India for being the first land to find the pathway to God. Hence, he exclaims the passage to India will bring about never-before-seen opportunities to connect with other people and traditions. He also celebrates the completion of the Pacific Railroad, which will tie the two coasts together, then returns his focus to the passage to India, and his intention to voyage there. But stopping there is not an option, and he declares he will "farther, farther, farther sail!"

Oldtown Folks

Characters in Harriet Beecher Stowe's "Oldtown Folks":
- Horace Holyoke
- Tina Percival
- Harry Percival
- Ellery Davenport
- Emily Rossiter

Horace Holyoke is the narrator in Harriet Beecher Stowe's "Oldtown Folks." Holyoke grew up in Oldtown, Massachusetts during the post-Revolutionary period. He explains in a famous preface that he will attempt to describe the events and the setting in a way that the reader will be able to see and hear the characteristic persons. Tina and Harry Percival are orphaned siblings, later discovered to be members of a wealthy British family. Horace falls in love with Tina, and Harry later becomes an Anglican clergyman. However, Tina marries Ellery Davenport, described as an aristocratic Revolutionary officer who resembles Aaron Burr. When it is discovered that Davenport fathered a child with Emily Rossiter, Tina adopts the child and goes to Europe with her husband. Davenport becomes a political leader and is killed in a duel. Two years later, Horace and Tina marry.

Poems and Prose

A Psalm of Life

1. Life is real! Life is earnest! And the grave is not its goal; Dust thou art, to dust returnest, Was not spoken of the soul.

2. Not enjoyment, and not sorrow, Is our destined end or way; But to act, that each tomorrow Find us farther than today.

3. Art is long, and Time is fleeting, And our hearts, though stout and brave, Still, like muffled drums, are beating Funeral marches to the grave.

In the first passage of Henry Wadsworth Longfellow's "A Psalm of Life," Longfellow is expressing that life can only truly be lived if one believes that the soul continues even when the body is dust. By stating "And the grave is not its goal," he is saying that that death is not the end, or the purpose of life. In the second passage, Longfellow states that we are to live life anticipating that the next day will be even better than the day before. In the third passage, Longfellow reminds the reader that art created during one's life will live on, long after its creator dies. Even though our hearts may be strong and courageous, they will eventually stop beating. Art can be interpreted as what one has done with life, and how that legacy will continue.

Because I Could Not Stop for Death

1. Because I could not stop for Death, He kindly stopped for me; The carriage held but just ourselves and Immortality.

2. We passed the school where children played, Their lessons scarcely done; We passed the fields of gazing grain, We passed the setting sun.

In these two stanzas of Emily Dickinson's "Because I Could Not Stop for Death," the characters include the narrator, death, immortality, and children. The narrator is a woman who calmly accepts death, even welcoming him. Death is the suitor who comes calling for the narrator to escort her to eternity. Immortality is a passenger in the carriage, and children are characters symbolizing early life. In the second passage, the school represents the morning of life or childhood, the fields represent the working years, or the midday of life, and the setting sun represents the evening of life, or dying.

Civil Disobedience

Throughout Henry David Thoreau's "Civil Disobedience" and in this passage, Thoreau attempts to persuade readers to oppose unjust government policies. He believes it is the duty of citizens to do so, and the power of the legislator should never replace one's conscience. After all, what purpose would a conscience serve if it is ignored? Thoreau believed that every human being has an inborn knowledge that enables him to recognize moral truth. Therefore, if government adopts a policy or law that is offensive to the conscience, it is the individual's responsibility to prevent the government from engaging in unjust conflicts and enacting immoral laws over man. Through civil disobedience, Thoreau believed we should oppose such policies, and even be willing to go to jail rather than yield to unethical government activities and laws.

When Lilacs Last in the Dooryard Bloom'd

When lilacs last in the dooryard bloom'd, And the great star early droop'd in the western sky in the night, I mourn'd, and yet shall mourn with ever-returning spring. Ever-returning spring, trinity sure to me you bring, Lilac blooming perennial and dropping star in the west, and Thought of him I love.

While most poets associate spring with resurrection and rebirth of life, Walt Whitman's pastoral elegy "When Lilacs Last in the Dooryard Bloom'd," declares this spring a time of deep mourning. Assassinated in April, a time when Easter is celebrated and spring is at its peak, Lincoln's tragic death overshadows a normally

- 18 -

happy time for both Whitman and the nation. In this passage, Whitman is expressing the depth of his grief. Although it is the time of "Lilac blooming perennial," Whitman is stating that he will always feel different than the last time the lilacs bloomed. The image of the Great Star that has "droop'd in the western sky" provides a personified image of a star that normally shines high, now heavy from the weight it is surely carrying during such a time. And even though spring will return again and again, Whitman envisions he will always mourn the loss of Lincoln despite the season's symbolism of new life.

Self-Reliance

The sentiment they instill is of more value than any thought they may contain. To believe your own thought, to believe that what is true for you in your private heart is true for all men, —that is genius. Speak your latent conviction, and it shall be the universal sense; for the inmost in due time becomes the outmost,—and our first thought is rendered back to us by the trumpets of the Last Judgment.

In Ralph Waldo Emerson's "Self-Reliance," this passage depicts the main message Emerson wishes to convey to his reader: to trust one's own intuition, to hear what is in your private heart, rather than following what is popular opinion, or trying to think like others who, often inaccurately, are viewed to be models of perfection. After all, it takes no thought to adopt the thoughts of others, but to listen to your own inner voice, and to think for yourself and not be afraid to express your own original ideas—that is genius. He encourages the reader that the conviction that comes from that inner sense, and not one that has been processed from hearing the opinions of others, is ultimately, our truth. We should speak this truth without being afraid, and take pride in our own unique individuality.

Moby Dick

In Herman Melville's *Moby Dick*, Captain Ahab seeks vengeance on the much-feared sperm whale, Moby Dick, to whom he lost his leg. He is obsessed with his quest for vengeance, to the detriment of all of those unfortunate enough to be whalers on his ship. Moby Dick represents the mysterious, impenetrable power that controls the world and manipulates our destinies. To some, this could be God, Satan, fate, or some other force. And even if Captain Ahab succeeds at harpooning Moby Dick, he can never obtain this great knowledge and power that only such a force holds. The whale's impact on the lives of human beings, like the whale himself, can never be captured and conquered. Even with the best attempt and near-success, it remains unattainable. Therefore, Moby Dick represents all of the forces working against Ahab, and can easily be understood by every human being as that something that we know exists, but over which we have no control.

To a Waterfowl

There is a Power whose care
Teaches thy way along that pathless coast—
The desert and illimitable air—
Lone wandering, but not lost.

In this passage from William Cullen Bryant's "To a Waterfowl," the author is stating that there is a higher, unseen power whose care for us teaches us how to find our way, even when no clear path exists, when the desert is expansive, and the air seemingly infinite. He is stating that although we sometimes travel alone, or feel alone and may wander, we are never lost. This poem, which depicts God guiding a waterfowl to his summer home, is a metaphor of how he guides us to our ultimate destination, the journey being life and the destination being heaven. It is a profession of faith in God, and trusting that he is there with us throughout this journey. We need only trust that he cares enough to bring us home safely, even when what's in front of us is not clear or well defined.

The Raven

1. Then this ebony bird beguiling my sad fancy into smiling,
By the grave and stern decorum of the countenance it wore.
"Though thy crest be shorn and shaven, thou," I said, "art sure no craven,
Ghastly grim and ancient raven wandering from the Nightly shore—
Tell me what thy lordly name is on the Night's Plutonian shore!"
Quoth the Raven, "Nevermore."

2. "Prophet!" said I, "thing of evil—prophet still, if bird or devil!
By that Heaven that bends above us—by that God we both adore—
Tell this soul with sorrow laden if, within
the distant Aidenn,
It shall clasp a sainted maiden whom the angels name Lenore—
Clasp a rare and radiant maiden whom the angels name Lenore."
Quoth the Raven, "Nevermore."

In Edgar Allan Poe's "The Raven," a man has lost his beloved, named Lenore. Lamenting her death and in deep mourning and depression, he reads a book of ancient stories to occupy his time on a cold winter night. He hears a persistent tapping on the window and discovers a raven, which flies in and lands above a door atop the bust of Pallas. In the first stanza, the speaker, who is aware of the raven's grim demeanor, asks its name, to which the Raven replies, "Nevermore." At first he believes this to be the raven's name, and begins to question it, only to find it continues to say "nevermore" to all of his thoughts. In the second stanza, he has begun to understand that what the raven is really telling him is that his sadness will never end, and he will never see his beloved Lenore ever again. He inquires if he will ever "clasp a sainted maiden" or "a rare and radiant maiden whom the angels named Lenore," to which the raven confirms his suspicion, replying, "Nevermore."

Nature

Standing on the bare ground, my head bathed by the blithe air, and uplifted into infinite space, all mean egotism vanishes. I become a transparent eye-ball. I am nothing. I see all. The currents of the Universal Being circulate through me; I am part or particle of God…" "…I am the lover of uncontained and immortal beauty.

Transcendentalism is a philosophy that emerged in the early to mid-19th century, and can be defined as any system of philosophy emphasizing the intuitive and spiritual above the empirical and material. In this passage from Ralph Waldo Emerson's "Nature," he is reflecting on his ability to see nature plainly, not superficially. He states that when he stands in the woods, he feels the "Universal Being" flowing through him, identifying God, a sentence that captures the essence of the transcendentalism philosophy. He suggests a paradoxical relationship between man and nature when he states, "I am nothing. I see all." Again, this is a recurrent theme in transcendental philosophy—one must lose himself before he can find himself.

Thanatopsis

1. When thoughts of the last bitter hour come like a blight over thy spirit, and sad images
Of the stern agony, and shroud, and pall, And breathless darkness, and the narrow house Make
Thee to shudder, and grow sick at heart, Go forth, under the open sky, and list To Nature's
Teachings…
2. Yet not to thine eternal resting-place Shalt thou retire alone, nor couldst thou wish
Couch more magnificent. Thou shalt lie down With patriarchs of the infant world, with kings,
The powerful of the earth, the wise, the good, Fair forms, and hoary seers of ages past,
All in one mighty sepulchre.

In the first passage of William Cullen Bryant's "Thanatopsis," the author is stating his belief that that nature will help guide its listener to an understanding of the cycle of life, death and rebirth. He is, in essence, instructing the reader to shun civilization and instead, pay close attention to the teachings of nature. In the second passage, Bryant is comforting the reader, ensuring him that, though death is certain, you will not die alone. Instead, it is the great equalizer, and you will be in the presence of and equal to kings, the powerful, the wise and the good. Again, he insists that by being a careful observer and listener of nature, you will have a better understanding of this fact. This poem illustrates many of the qualities of Romantic era writings, contemplating nature as a path to spiritual and moral development.

Ichabod

John Greenleaf Whittier penned "Ichabod" after the death of Daniel Webster, who, to Whittier's great disappointed, supported the Fugitive Slave Bill allowing new slave states to enter the union. Interpret from the following passages how Whittier is asking his fellows to treat the now deceased Webster, and explain to which Biblical story the last passage is referring.

1. Let not the land once proud of him insult him now, Nor brand with deeper shame his dim, Dishonored brow. But let its humbled sons, instead, From sea to lake, A long lament, as for the dead, In sadness make.

2. Then pay the reverence of old days To his dead fame; Walk backward, with averted gaze
And hide the shame!

Though extremely disappointed by Webster's political decision, John Greenleaf Whittier remembers the time when he believed him to be a great senator. The Hebrew translation of the name "Ichabod" is inglorious, hence the title of the poem. In the above passage, Whittier is reminding his readers that that Ichabod/Webster once was a man of whom the country was proud, and in death, it would not be appropriate to respond in anger, thereby deepening his shame and dishonor. In the last passage, he makes a plea to be respectful of the old days, and the time when Ichabod/Webster was a highly respected political figure. And as Noah's sons walked backward with their eyes averted from their drunken father's shameful nakedness, he too instructs his readers to respectfully walk away and look away from the shame of this inglorious political decision.

The Last Leaf

1. They say that in his prime, Ere the *pruning-knife* of Time Cut him down...

2. The *mossy marbles* rest On the lips that he has prest In their bloom...

3. And if I should live to be *The last leaf* upon the tree In the spring...

In "The Last Leaf," Oliver Wendell Holmes makes powerful use of several metaphors. In the first line, "pruning-knife" is a metaphor for time. Time is described as a weapon that injures the body, not instantly fatal, but weakening and deforming the body as it whittles away at life a little bit at a time. In the second line, "mossy marbles" are used to describe the old man's teeth. Instead of being sharp, they are now merely rounded and therefore useless, due to the toll time takes on every part of the body. In the third line, from which the poem gets its title, "the last leaf" upon the tree in spring is compared to the old man. He too is the last leaf, being the last surviving member of his family, who have died before him and are now ground into the dirt like fallen leaves. The other people bloomed and thrived at the same time he did, but now he is out of place in this new season of spring, which is making way for a new generation.

Hope is the Thing with Feathers

1. Hope is the thing with feathers
That perches in the soul,
And sings the tune—without the words,
And never stops at all,

2. And sweetest in the gale is heard;
And sore must be the storm
That could abash the little bird
That kept so many warm.

3. I've heard it in the chillest land,
And on the strangest sea;
Yet, never, in extremity,
It asked a crumb of me.

In the first stanza of Emily Dickinson's "Hope is the Thing with Feathers," hope is a "thing" because it is a feeling, and that feeling is like a bird. Whatever is being said of the bird applies to hope. The bird "sings the tune without the words." This begs the question, is hope a matter of words, or is it a wordless feeling about the future? She conveys that hope is always present and always possible. In stanza two, she ponders whether we need hope more when things are going well or when things are going badly. *Sore* means "severe" and only the most extreme conditions could affect this bird, this hope. If the bird is "abashed" what would happen to the individual's hope? In stanza three, even in the coldest land, hope kept the individual warm. The bird, faithful and unabashed, follows and sings to the speaker under the worst circumstances. "Yet" even in the most critical circumstances the bird never asked for even a "crumb" in return for its support.

I Saw in Louisiana a Live-oak Growing

I saw in Louisiana a live-oak growing, All alone stood it and the moss hung down from the branches, Without any companion it grew there uttering joyous leaves of dark green, And its look, rude, unbending, lusty, made me think of myself, But I wonder'd how it could utter joyous leaves standing alone there without its friend near, for I knew I could not. And I broke off a twig with a certain number of leaves upon it, and twined around it a little moss, And brought it away and I have placed it in sight in my room, It is not needed to remind me as of my own dear friends, (For I believe lately I think of little else than of them,) Yet it remains to me a curious token, it makes me think of manly love; For all that, and though the live-oak glistens there in Louisiana solitary in a wide flat space, Uttering joyous leaves all its life without a friend a lover near, I know very well I could not.

A poem about the human condition, Walt Whitman is expressing his need for other people, and perhaps not just other people, but similar people and close friends. Although he admires the oak for its strength, its ability to provide "joyous leaves of dark green" without a friend nearby, he admits this is not something he could do. In fact, he is expressing that in separation, he could not create, nor be creative, unlike the lone oak tree . The twig he breaks off the tree "with a certain number of leaves upon it," will serve as a reminder to him of his need for people—not because he needs reminding to think of his friends, but it reminds him of mankind's need for companionship and love, and the contrast between the tree and human beings.

I Heard a Fly Buzz When I Died

I heard a fly buzz when I died; The stillness round my form
Was like the stillness in the air between the heaves of storm
The eyes beside had wrung them dry, And breaths were gathering sure
For that last onset, when the king be witnessed in his power.
I willed my keepsakes, signed away what portion of me I
Could make assignable,—and then there interposed a fly,
With blue, uncertain, stumbling buzz, Between the light and me;
And then the windows failed, and then I could not see to see.

Emily Dickinson's "I Heard a Fly Buzz When I Died" describes the painless, yet horrifying death of the narrator. The people surrounding her are silent and their grief exhausted, as described when she says, "the eyes beside had wrung them dry." There is a stillness in the air, a moment of expectation, except for the distinct sound of the fly's buzzing. The narrator has given away "my keepsakes," indicating she is ready for death. And though it is "the king/Be witnessed in his power" who is expected, the fly, ironically, appears instead. The fly could be interpreted as death. Flies are associated with the decay of death, feeding on dead flesh. If this is so, the suggestion might be that death is simply physical decay with no spiritual significance. The fly could also be interpreted as "lord of the flies," Beelzebub. If this were so, perhaps the "king" the narrator is waiting for could actually be Satan. Therefore, different interpretations of the fly itself could significantly alter the poem's meaning.

The Philosophy of Composition

1. There is a distinct limit to all works of literary art—the limit of one sitting.

2. Most writers would "positively shudder at letting the public take a peep behind the scenes... at the fully matured fancies discarded in despair... at the cautious selections and rejections.

- 24 -

3. ...it is clear that the brevity must be in direct ratio of the intensity of the intended effect... that a certain degree of duration is absolutely requisite for the production of any effect at all.

Based on "The Philosophy of Composition," Poe believed that when it came to length, all literary works should be short, especially poetry. He also notes that the short story is superior to the novel for this reason. For the second element, method, Poe dismissed the notion of artistic intuition. He argues that writing is methodical and analytical, not spontaneous. He declares that no other author has admitted this because most would "positively shudder" at allowing the public to see how methodically their "artistic" creation actually came about. As for unity of effect, Poe believed that a work of fiction should be written only after the author has decided how it will end, based on which emotional response he wishes to create. Poe believed the death of a beautiful woman was by far the most poetic topic, particularly when written from the perspective of the bereaved lover, a theme apparent in many of his works.

The Birthmark

Nathaniel Hawthorne's "The Birthmark
You came so nearly perfect from the hand of Nature that this slightest possible defect, which we hesitate whether to term a defect or a beauty, shocks me, as being the visible mark of earthly perfection.
But seeing her otherwise so perfect, he found this one defect grow more and more intolerable with every moment of their united lives. It was the fatal flaw of humanity which Nature, in one shape or another, stamps ineffaceably on all her productions, either to imply that they are temporary and finite, or that their perfection must be wrought by toil and pain.

In the above passages from Nathaniel Hawthorne's "The Birthmark," Alymer is referring to the birthmark on the cheek of his beloved wife, Georgiana, which is in the shape of a small red hand. Being a great scientist who believes in man's ultimate control over nature, he is extremely shocked and troubled that such perfection could have this "defect." Though he loves her and sees her as "otherwise perfect," his obsession with the imperfection consumes his thoughts, and as a man of science, he wishes to remove the birthmark. Although he eventually succeeds at removing it, his wife passes away simultaneously with the disappearance of the birthmark. This poses philosophical questions still highly applicable today: What is perfection and is it even possible in the physical state? Just because man can accomplish something, should he? It reveals that when man tries to accomplish what he was not intended to, disaster will be the ultimate result.

Lenore

1. Ah, broken is the golden bowl!—the spirit flown forever!
Let the bell toll!—a saintly soul floats on the Stygian river:
And, Guy de Vere, hast thou no tear? —weep now or never more!
See! on yon drear and rigid bier low lies thy love, Lenore!
Come! let the burial rite be read—the funeral song be sung! —
An anthem for the queenliest dead that ever died so young—
A dirge for her the doubly dead in that she died so young.
2. Wretches! ye loved her for her wealth and hated her for her pride;
And when she fell in feeble health, ye blessed her—that she died!
How shall the ritual, then, be read? —the requiem how be sung
By you—by yours, the evil eye, —by yours, the slanderous tongue
That did to death the innocence that died, and died so young?

In stanza one of Edgar Allan Poe's "Lenore," the speaker, possibly just an acquaintance of Lenore, announces her death, and asks that the bell toll for her as her soul floats toward the afterlife. He then states that Lenore's lover, Guy de Vere, should weep for her as she has passed and her funeral awaits. He then directs that the funeral begin, and asks the mourners to sing "a dirge" for this woman who died at such a young age. In stanza two, her lover Guy de Vere lashes out at the speaker and the other mourners, exclaiming that they only pretended to love her for her money, but secretly hated her for her pride. He accuses them of happiness and hope of her death when she became ill. He then asks how funeral rites can take place when such hypocrites and slanderers are among them, and who contributed to the death of one so young.

Historical and Social Settings

Old Ironsides

Oliver Wendell Holmes's poem "Old Ironsides" appeared in September of 1830 in response to a report in the Boston Daily Advertiser that the Navy was planning to scrap the USS Constitution, the oldest commissioned naval vessel afloat in the world, which captured numerous merchant ships and defeated five British warships. A public outcry arose and Holmes immediately penned this famous poem. After it was published, there was claim that the report was inaccurate, and that there were no plans to demolish the ship. However, this poem is nonetheless credited with saving it, thus representing that in such a case, the pen did prove to be mightier than the sword.

Annabel Lee and Romeo and Juliet

Couples in Edgar Allan Poe's "Annabel Lee" and Shakespeare's *Romeo and Juliet*
Like Romeo and Juliet, the couple in Edgar Allan Poe's poem, "Annabel Lee," are very young and very much in love. And like Shakespeare's star-crossed lovers, Poe's become victims of forces beyond their control, when Annabel Lee becomes ill and dies. They are also alike in that their love is eternal. Though Annabel Lee has passed, her young lover, the narrator of the poem, still loves her, as their souls are united, just as were Romeo and Juliet's. Poe's lovers also experience a love that is so great, others become resentful and jealous, in this case, the angels in heaven, whom her lover blames for making her ill and taking her away from him. Unlike Romeo and Juliet, who both die, Annabel Lee's lover remains, but sees his beloved whenever he looks toward the heavens at the moon and the stars.

The Oregon Trail

Before he became the first great chronicler of the American Frontier, Francis Parkman headed west in 1846 to follow the trail of the pioneers making their way to Oregon and California. When he reached the Rocky Mountains, Parkman and his party turned south, traveled down the Front Range, and returned via the Santa Fe Trail to Missouri. *The Oregon Trail* is filled with countless adventures clearly enjoyed by Parkman, who, during his journey, was lost, near starvation, and narrowly escaped Indian war parties. More than 150 years after its publication, *The Oregon Trail* remains a popular favorite in adventure stories, and was listed among the best adventure books in Adventure Magazine's Top 100 classics list. It remains a great source about the Western Frontier and the many uses of the Oregon Trail.

Romanticism authors

Settling into an established government, the mid-1800s allowed time for art and culture to flourish. Lofty ideals of democracy established in the previous century created a window for opportunity, while tension over inequality, particularly that of women and slaves, set the stage for creative release. Rising affluence in the nation led to more people developing and appreciating the skills of reading and writing, while also providing another popular theme of Romanticism: the downside of materialistic values and the inequities within a wealthy society. It was also a time when society looked for paths of spiritual fulfillment other than that of the Puritans, bringing about pantheism, while inspiration and emotion replaced more conventional literary forms, as Romantics believed the heart, not rules, was essential to good literature. The era of Romanticism reflected the political tone, shift in ideals, and healthy economic status of the mid-1800s, providing new opportunities that broke the confines of previous literary works. Three famous authors were Ralph Waldo Emerson, Edgar Allan Poe, and Nathaniel Hawthorne.

Nathaniel Hawthorne

Nathaniel Hawthorne's Puritan background was perhaps the greatest influence on his work. Colonel John Hawthorne, Nathaniel's great-grandfather, was the presiding judge in the Salem Witch Trials, and Hawthorne lived out most of his life in Salem. He later added the "w" to his last name to distance himself from the evils of his ancestors. The Puritan setting is utilized by Hawthorne in many of his tales, and Puritanical themes abound as well, such as guilt, isolationism and the idea of fate versus free will. Hawthorne's belief in the existence of the devil is also indicative of his Puritan background, as is determinism, also known as predestination. His somber outlook on living, his thorough analysis of the mind, and his own tendency to withdraw from society reflected his Puritan beliefs. However, unlike his Puritan ancestors, Hawthorne revealed compassion for sinners, and believed in the concept of "degrees of sin."

Literary Devices

The Fall of the House of Usher

By carefully selecting every word and every phrase, Edgar Allan Poe creates an overall tone of horror in "The Fall of the House of Usher." "Clouds hung oppressively low in the heavens," "a singularly dreary tract of country," and "the melancholy House of Usher" provide vivid imagery that sets the tone as one of dread, mystery, terror and morbidity. The fungus-ridden mansion is one example of how Poe uses symbolism, with the decrepit state of the mansion representing the decline of the Usher family. A second example occurs at the end of the story with the total collapse of the Usher mansion. This collapse, which occurs after the horrific deaths of the mansion's inhabitants, brother and sister Roderick and Madeline Usher, represents the fall of the Usher family, as their demise ends the Usher lineage.

I'm Nobody! Who Are You?

I'm nobody! Who are you?
Are you nobody, too?
Then there's a pair of us—don't tell!
They'd banish us, you know.

How dreary—to be somebody!
How public, like a frog.
To tell your name the livelong day
To an admiring bog!

Typical for Dickinson, these two stanzas are written in loose iambic trimeter, with occasional stress on the fourth syllable, e.g., "To tell your name the livelong day." It follows an ABCB rhyme scheme, and a dash is used in the first stanza to deliberately

- *28* -

interrupt the flow, another Dickinson trademark. Perhaps Dickinson is most famous for being not famous at all in her life, making this poem one of her greatest literary self-ironies. She published less than ten of her 1,800 written poems, and this poem demonstrates the kind of privacy she favored. It clearly states that in her opinion, it is far preferable to be a nobody—a luxury in fact—than to be a dreary somebody, who must make a concerted effort to croak like a frog in order to maintain a place in the spotlight, something Dickinson in no way did in her own life.

Realism and Naturalism (1870–1910)

The Portrait of a Lady

Henry James's *The Portrait of a Lady*, tells the story of Isabel Archer, who was raised to be independent. In America, Isabel refuses the hand of suitor Caspar Goodwood, and in Europe, she refuses a second proposal from aristocrat Lord Warburton, due to her fear of losing her independence. When in Europe, Isabel receives an inheritance from her uncle, Mr. Touchett, and is instantly befriended by Madame Merle, who takes her to Rome and introduces her to Gilbert Osmond. She marries Osmond, who treats her with coldness and contempt. Out of social and moral obligation, and a love for Osmond's daughter Pansy, Isabel chooses to remain in the marriage. She later discovers it is her "friend" Madame Merle who is Pansy's mother, with whom he still has a relationship. When her beloved cousin dies, she goes to England but promises Pansy she will return to Rome, which she does, despite an opportunity to run away with Caspar Goodwood.

The Awakening

Edna Pontellier is the main character in Kate Chopin's *The Awakening*. Always a romantic, newly married Edna believes that marriage is the end of passion and the beginning of responsibility. She suppresses her romantic, rebellious nature for a while, but her latent desires surface as she seeks an identity independent of her husband and children. She goes to Grand Isle, where she meets Robert Lebrun, and begins to see the world around her as a place to satisfy all of her own passions, without regard to consequences. She leaves her children in the care of their grandmother, and seems to have no remorse for any of her choices. In the end, Edna commits suicide, but it is left up to the reader to determine if Edna was a coward afraid to face life's difficulties, or someone who simply refused to bow to traditional conventions. Although Edna's actions are selfish, Chopin does not condemn her as such, but leaves it open for the reader to decide.

The Country of the Pointed Firs

In Sarah Orne Jewett's *The Country of the Pointed Firs*, the entire novel focuses on the description of the tiny community of Dunnet Landing. Mrs. Todd, the central character, serves as a touchstone by which the narrator interconnects the people of this community. The narrator meets or hears of many members of the community through Mrs. Todd, and learns of their relationships to one another. Although most of the people she meets—all of whom are over the age of 60 and are either widowed or widowers—seem to lead generally solitary lives, the strong community ties that hold Dunnet Landing together are clearly indicated. This is especially true of the Bowden family reunion, which demonstrates most powerfully the citizens' strong communal ties. This story weaves imagery with realistic conversations and stories, resulting in fiction that seems hardly fictional in the way it captures community ties.

The Rise of Silas Lapham

The Rise of Silas Lapham is a rags-to-riches story about the materialistic rise of Silas Lapham. Although Silas earns a fortune in the paint business, he lacks social standards, which he tries to attain through his daughter's marriage to Tom Corey, one of Boston's "old money" families. This novel was one of the first to focus on the American businessman, but also depicts the relatively new societal clash between the old rich, "new money," and the differences that tend to pit them against each other. Though many old fortunes have somewhat diminished, and though the newly rich are often wealthier, they try desperately to emulate the manners and customs of their far more cultured predecessors. But despite what Silas lacks in social standards, he reveals through his business decisions that he has something much more valuable—honesty and integrity, even at the expense of his business and newly acquired wealth.

McTeague

In Frank Norris's novel *McTeague*, Norris reveals the corrupting influence of gold on the central couple in the story, McTeague and his wife, Trina. Before they marry, Trina wins $5000 in a lottery. Envious of their good fortune, Marcus Schouler, McTeague's friend, informs the police that McTeague is practicing as a dentist without a license or degree. McTeague loses his practice, and forced to live in poor quarters, Trina becomes mean and bitter. When she refuses to share her money, which she has stashed away, McTeague beats her to death in a fit of fury. He runs away to escape prosecution, but Schouler captures him and chains him to his own body. McTeague kills Schouler in a brutal fight, and he is left stranded in the desert handcuffed to the corpse of his enemy. Norris provides symbolism with gold objects throughout the story, including a golden canary cage in McTeague's room, McTeague's birthday present from Trina, and a giant tooth coated with French gilt used in his dentist establishment.

The Education of Henry Adams

In Henry Adams's *The Education of Henry Adams*, the author begins with an exploration of his youth, and the shoes he had to fill. His great-grandfather was second U.S. president John Adams, and his grandfather was sixth U.S. president John Quincy Adams. Adams recalls his strict, rule-dominant winters in Boston, contrasted with the summers he relished in Quincy that brought freedom, hope and a close relationship with his grandfather. Though he later attended Harvard, and had access to the best that Boston could offer, the author adopted the attitude that his education had been useless for dealing with the rapidly changing pattern of his age. Henry protests the limits of formal education, believing too much emphasis was placed on memorizing, and too little on intellectual curiosity. He sought first-hand knowledge of music and art, and said of formal education, "The chief wonder of education is that it does not ruin everybody concerned in it, teachers and taught."

Editha

William Dean Howells, a voice of pacifism, depicts war as traumatic and dehumanizing. This is in direct contrast to the title character in "Editha," who has a romanticized idea of war and refers to it as "glorious." Editha is a young girl who believes that her boyfriend is not a real man unless he goes to fight for his country. She bullies him into enlisting in the army when war is declared, and he is among the first wave of soldiers who are killed. Out of respect, Editha dresses in mourning black, but also with a great deal of pride. When she visits Mrs. Gearson, George's mother, Mrs. Gearson lashes out, telling her that she would rather her son be killed than live with the blood of other soldiers on his hands. When having her portrait painted, Editha confides this exchange to the artist, who tells Editha the mother was "vulgar," lifting Editha's guilt, and allowing her to return to a life of living in the ideal.

The Outcasts of Poker Flat

In Poker Flat, California, an effort to "cleanse" the town of bad elements results in four "immoral" characters' exile: gambler John Oakhurst, "The Duchess"—a saloon girl, brothel owner "Mother Shipton," and suspected robber Uncle Billy. Halfway to their destination, they meet Piney Woods and Tom Simpson, a young runaway couple who plan to marry. Tom leads them to a hut, where they spend the night. A bad snowstorm comes, and Oakhurst awakens to find Uncle Billy has stolen their mules. Mother Shipton soon dies, having secretly saved her provisions for Piney. Simpson goes for help, but when the "law of Poker Flat" later arrives at the hut, Duchess and Piney are dead in an embrace, and Oakhurst, "the strongest and yet the weakest of the outcasts," has committed suicide. Above his head a note reads: "BENEATH THIS TREE LIES THE BODY OF JOHN OAKHURST, WHO STRUCK A STREAK OF BAD LUCK ON THE 23D OF NOVEMBER, 1850, AND HANDED IN HIS CHECKS ON THE 7TH DECEMBER, 1850."

The Boarded Window

"The Boarded Window," by Ambrose Bierce, tells the tale of Murlock, an elderly, humorless man who lived alone in the wilderness in an isolated cabin that had a boarded window. The narrator tells the story of a young, married Murlock, whose wife became ill and ceased to move or breathe. A distraught Murlock laid her body on their table, and customarily tied her wrists together with ribbon. Next to her, he fell asleep until he was awakened in the middle of the night by a fearsome noise. After prolonged scuffling noises and confusion erupted, Murlock shot his rifle aimlessly, only to see an enormous panther dragging his wife toward the open window. Murlock fainted, and when he came to, the panther was gone. However, the ribbon that bound his wife's wrists was broken. Her hands were tightly clenched, and between her teeth was a fragment of the panther's ear. The twist begs the question, was she dead or still alive when the panther made his attack?

An Occurrence at Owl Creek Bridge

Set during the American Civil War, Ambrose Bierce's "An Occurrence at Owl Creek Bridge" tells the story of Peyton Farquhar, a Confederate sympathizer condemned to hang at the Owl Creek Bridge. While waiting to drop, he thinks of his wife and children and imagines escaping and returning home to them. As the story plays out, it appears this is exactly what happens, but in the end, the reader learns it was all imagined between the moment he dropped until his neck was broken. Bierce hints at this by portraying Farquhar's senses as being extremely heightened, being able to see bugs on leaves and individual blades of grass despite swirling around in the river. Secondly, the description of his effort to free his wrists depicts Farquhar as an interested observer, rather than a participant in his struggle for life. Thirdly, he refers to entering "unknown country," that being death, which we enter alone and only once.

Bras Coupé in George Washington Cable's The Grandissimes

Retold several times, the story of Bras Coupé in George Washington Cable's The Grandissimes tells the story of an affluent, vibrant New Orleans society that remains tainted by the atrocities of slavery. Within the Grandissime family, there are those who would like to end slavery—even if that results in erasing Creole culture, and those who hold tightly to racist ways to preserve the Grandissime "way of life." Bras Coupé is an enslaved African prince who lives on a Spanish Creole plantation. Angered by the indignity of his plight, he attacks his white overseer and is viciously pursued and eventually beaten to death and mutilated by a mob. Bras Coupé personifies the cruelty of slavery, and reveals the level of degeneracy still alive in so-called genteel southern society. What happens to Bras Coupé illustrates that such privilege is often begotten at great human cost.

A White Heron

Sarah Orne Jewett's A White Heron tells the story of nine-year-old Sylvia, who has moved from the city to live in the New England woods with her grandmother, Mrs. Tilley. Sylvia relishes the newfound freedom she feels from living in the country, and discovers a love of nature. Every night, she enjoys walking the cow, Mistress Mooly, home from the fields. One evening, when returning with Mistress Mooly, she encounters a hunter who offers a large sum of money if she can direct him to a rare white heron that he wishes to shoot and preserve for his collection. She searches for the bird herself so she can lead the hunter to it, but when she discovers the white heron, she is so moved by its beauty, and the view of wildlife from atop a tall tree, she does not disclose its whereabouts. Sylvia gives up a monetary reward to save the white heron, but has gained an understanding and satisfaction from nature that exceeds monetary value.

Under the Lion's Paw

"Under the Lion's Paw," by Hamlin Garland, is the story of the Haskins family and their plight to buy farmland. Eaten out by grasshoppers in western Kansas, they travel to Iowa, where they set to work on a farm they intend to purchase, owned by Jim Butler. The Haskins put all of their efforts into working the farm for three long years, and are finally prepared to buy it. However, Butler notes the increased value of the farm, and establishes a higher price, which Haskins is not able to afford. Although angered enough to kill Butler, Haskins refrains in the interest of his wife and daughters. The title "Under the Lion's Paw" is a description of Jim Haskins at the end of the story, sitting alone, crushed under the paw of the "lion" of land speculation.

The Open Boat

Characters in Stephen Crane's "The Open Boat":
- The Captain
- The Cook
- The Correspondent
- The Oiler

In Stephen Crane's "The Open Boat," the Captain is the character in charge of the "dinghy" that keeps the men afloat after they are shipwrecked. True to captain form, he believes it is his duty to keep the men safe and ensure they reach land. The Cook, talkative and optimistic, is described as fat and "untidily dressed." Though he does not help with the rowing, he bails water out of the boat to help keep it afloat. The Correspondent is based on the author, who himself was shipwrecked off the Florida coast when working as a war correspondent. The Oiler, named Billie, is strong and seems the most likely of the characters to survive. However, he is the only one who does not survive, drowning just off shore. It could be said that Nature is the main character, as it controls their fate throughout the story.

The Red Badge of Courage

In Stephen Crane's *The Red Badge of Courage*, the red badge—a blood stain—symbolizes the courage of soldiers. In the case of the main character, Henry Fleming, however, the blood stain is a symbol of cowardice, as Henry received the "badge" from his fight with another union solider after deserting. The flag, too, symbolizes

- 33 -

the courage of the person who carried it, since the flag bearer must always stand at the front lines. Though Henry intended to desert the army, he finds his way back to his regiment with the help of another soldier. He lies about his wound from the fight, saying it is from battle, and no one suspects his attempt to desert. The following day, he goes above and beyond in his displays of courage, fighting at the front lines and encouraging his fellow soldiers to keep fighting. Though complimented by his Colonel, he has feelings of guilt for his attempt at desertion.

The Call of the Wild

In Jack London's *The Call of the Wild*, Buck, a large dog who looks similar to a wolf, leads a comfortable life with his owner in the Santa Clara Valley of Northern California. Stolen and sold to a trainer of sled dogs, Buck is forced to adapt to his new, harsh life, pulling sleds with other dogs and fighting for his survival. After defeating his nemesis, Spitz, in a fight, he becomes the leader of the sled team. After his ordeal, he changes hands several times between incompetent owners, and is nearly starved and beaten to death. Eventually he finds security once again with his kind and loving owner, John Thornton. Thornton, however, is killed by Yeehat Indians, and Buck, in a rage, kills several members of the tribe. He turns back to the wild and enters a sort of dream world, one where he becomes The Ghost Dog, something of a legend.

The Good Anna

Anna Federner, described by Gertrude Stein in "The Good Anna," is of "solid lower middle-class south German stock." She works as a housekeeper for Miss Mathilda, and is by far the authority in the household. Part One depicts her five years with Miss Mathilda, and the iron hand with which she rules everyone—her underservants as well as Miss Mathilda herself. But she does so with protectiveness, as Miss Mathilda has a tendency to give away money indiscriminately. Part Two provides the background of Anna, who shows a track record for being determined and willful, getting her way in most things, and yet, generous to a fault. She also has power struggles in friendship, stating, "In friendship, power always has its downward curve." Part Three chronicles Anna's last years, living in the house Miss Mathilda has left her. She fails to charge adequate boarding rates, and works too much, which weakens her. Her only remaining friend, Mrs. Drehten, convinces her to have an operation, from which Anna dies.

The Wonderful Tar-Baby Story

Intent on catching Br'er Rabbit for dinner, Br'er Fox sets a clever trap on the side of the road: a tar-baby that will easily entrap the rabbit if there is any physical contact. Br'er Rabbit stops to talk to the tar-baby, and becomes incensed when the "baby" does not respond, ignoring "respectubble folks" like himself. Just as Br'er Fox had hoped, Br'er Rabbit strikes out at the tar-baby and instantly becomes entangled in the black tar. Br'er Fox makes his appearance on the side of the road and hints that

Br'er Rabbit will be his dinner. The reader learns later from the telling of the story by Uncle Remus that the rabbit narrowly escaped due to his trickery. He begs Br'er Fox to do anything but throw him in the "brier-patch." Br'er Fox does just this, and it allows Br'er Rabbit to escape. In the case of both characters, a moral lesson is revealed about the dangers and downfalls of adopting an attitude of superiority over another.

The Real Thing

89b) "The Real Thing," by Henry James, portrays a genuine aristocratic couple, the Monarchs, who, down on their luck, are hired as models by the narrator, an aspiring painter and illustrator. Though the narrator believes they will suit his work perfectly, because after all, they are "the real thing," instead he disappointedly finds them to be inflexible for his work. This point is especially driven home when Jack Hawley, a friend and fellow artist, criticizes the work depicting the Monarchs, suggesting that they may have permanently hurt the narrator's art. This is the story's first irony. The second occurs when it turns out that the perfect models for his aristocratic art are two lower-class people, Oronte, a flashy but versatile Italian model, and Miss Churm, a lower-class British woman who has the gift of portraying anyone of any class quite convincingly.

A Modern Instance

A Modern Instance, by William Dean Howells, tells the sad tale of Marcia Gaylord and Bartley Hubbard, a young couple who meet in a Maine village, and elope to Boston after a brief courtship. The story begins on the promising note of marriage, and the narrative proceeds to track its gradual decline. Parents, religion, and the social hierarchy of Boston fail to provide anything that might help salvage the Hubbards' marriage. Even after the birth of a daughter, they continue to struggle until Bartley abandons his wife and child. His dishonesty as a journalist leads to his mortal end, when he is shot after smearing a prominent citizen with a story he knows to be false. Marcia is left abandoned and bitter, and the reader is left asking many modern-day questions: How can such "instances" be prevented, and what can be done to ensure society's institutions are equipped to help couples such as the Hubbards? The lawyer Atherton answers these questions in the last words of the novel: "I don't know."

The Man That Corrupted Hadleyburg

Hadleyburg is a town that takes great pride in its reputation for being honest and "incorruptible." When a passing stranger is offended by its people, he vows to corrupt the town. He tempts them by leaving a bag of gold at the house of Mr. and Mrs. Richards, claiming that a man in town gave him life-changing advice 20 years prior. Whoever correctly writes down this advice at a public meeting will receive the gold. Everyone in town receives a letter telling them the answer. All of them, including Mr. and Mrs. Richards, submit this given answer, exposing them for their lie. Everyone is humiliated, but Mr. and Mrs. Richards's note is never read. Proclaimed to be the only upstanding couple, the stranger gives them $40,000, claiming that Mr. Richards once gave him invaluable advice. Guilt-ridden, Mr. and Mrs. Richards become ill and confess before dying. Hadleyburg, embarrassed by the exposure, changes its name and once again becomes an honest town—"and the man will have to rise early that catches it napping again."

Life on the Mississippi

Life on the Mississippi is Mark Twain's personal story of life on the river. Starting out in life as a cub steamboat pilot under Horace Bixby, Twain learns how to navigate the treacherous river. After getting his own license, he begins to pilot on his own, and experiences many adventures along the way, while meeting many interesting people. His career as a steamboat pilot ended in 1861 due to the Civil War. The second part jumps to 1882, when Twain has a chance to take steamships from St. Louis to New Orleans and back up the river to Minnesota. The first part of the book takes place during the pre-Civil War era, and the second part takes place afterward, providing ample commentary about life in America after the Civil War, and reflections about the differences between the North and the South.

Plain Language from Truthful James

Bret Harte's "Plain Language from Truthful James" or "The Heathen Chinee" is a narrative poem about two "city slickers," Bill Nyes and Honest James, who entice immigrant Ah Sin into a card game. Though they intend to cheat him of all his money, Ah Sin is a card shark who foils the plot and beats them at their own game. They react with violence, reflecting true-to-life situations and attitudes prevalent toward immigrants in San Francisco at that time. While the real-life Nyes and Honest James used this poem to promote their crusade against immigrants, Harte intended the poem to be a satire of this prejudice, and was appalled to learn that his work was being quoted as something other than a parody of hypocrisy. Harte himself was active in crusading against bigotry toward Native Americans and immigrants, and in later years, regretted ever writing the poem.

The Country of the Pointed Firs

The Country of the Pointed Firs, by Sarah Orne Jewett, takes place in Dunnet Landing, a fictional shipping and fishing village in coastal Maine. The story depicts a writer from Boston who has rented a room for the summer in the home of Mrs. Todd. Dunnet Landing is mainly populated by elderly men and women of the shipping industry, which declined significantly after the Civil War as industrialization began to develop. As the writer gains their trust, she begins to hear the many stories of the locals about the town, sea, and families in the community, revealing the complex layers that exist underneath this quaint, quiet village. Three themes found in *The Country of the Pointed Firs* include nostalgia of the people, strong community ties, and perhaps most of all, the bond between women: mothers, daughters and friends.

The Turn of the Screw

"The Turn of the Screw," by Henry James, is a ghost story revolving around the lives of a governess, a housekeeper named Mrs. Grose, and two recently orphaned children, Miles and Flora. A governess is hired by the children's indifferent uncle to care for them at a country home. Flora is currently being cared for by Mrs. Grose, and Miles has just been expelled from boarding school for an unknown reason. Almost immediately, the housekeeper begins to see apparitions, first a man and then a woman. She hesitates, but finally tells Mrs. Grose, who confirms from her description that it is Peter Quint, a former valet now deceased. The woman is Miss Jessel, her dead predecessor. Though the governess suspects the children see these apparitions as well, they will not admit it. The story has spurred much debate about whether the ghosts are real, or if the governess's sanity is in question.

Poems and Prose

We Wear the Mask

We wear the mask that grins and lies,
It hides our cheeks and shades our eyes,—
This debt we pay to human guile;
With torn and bleeding hearts we smile,
And mouth with myriad subtleties.
Why should the world be over-wise,
In counting all our tears and sighs?
Nay, let them only see us, while
We wear the mask.
We smile, but, O great Christ, our cries
To thee from tortured souls arise.
We sing, but oh the clay is vile
Beneath our feet, and long the mile;
But let the world dream otherwise,
We wear the mask!

Though Paul Laurence Dunbar's poem, "We Wear the Mask," can easily apply to all human beings' tendency to disguise or "mask" pain and sadness, it is most likely directed particularly at slavery, and the mask of pain and sadness forced upon African-American slaves. In the first stanza, he depicts the mask as a liar, hiding true emotions due to the humiliation and disrespect endured by the slaves, the "debt we pay to human guile." In the second stanza, he says it is better not to let the world, or the slave masters, see their true sorrows, but only what the mask presents. Perhaps this was out of pride, and not wanting to give them satisfaction in knowing the agony the slaves truly felt. Or, perhaps the mask hid their fear of being treated worse if they revealed their human emotions. The third stanza depicts the slaves' deep spirituality. They realized that Christ understood their suffering, so it is only to him that they allow their "tortured souls" to be revealed, while the world embraced indifference.

Do Not Weep, Maiden, For War Is Kind

Do not weep, maiden, for war is kind,
Because your lover threw wild hands toward the sky
And the affrighted steed ran on alone,
Do not weep.
War is kind.
Hoarse, booming drums of the regiment,
Little souls who thirst for fight,
These men were born to drill and die.
The unexplained glory flies above them.
Great is the battle-god, great, and his kingdom—
A field where a thousand corpses lie.

The title of Stephen Crane's "Do Not Weep, Maiden, For War Is Kind" establishes irony, which continues in the first stanza. This stanza addresses the lover of a soldier who has died in battle, telling her not to weep, and presenting a melodramatic image of that death. The image of the rider-less horse galloping away from its fallen owner has become a staple of Western movies. In the second stanza, the images provided are more generalized, depicting the drums of the regiment, eager young soldiers ready to battle to the death, the flag flying overhead, and a battlefield "where a thousand corpses lie." This stanza is meant to underscore Crane's condescending attitude toward war, the military, and the soldiers who are fighting. By stating "these men were born to drill and die," he notes the futility of their purpose. The contrast reveals that, although Crane condemns the military as a whole (stanza two), he is sympathetic to individual victims and the loved ones they leave behind (stanza one).

Miniver Cheevy

Miniver Cheevy, child of scorn, Grew lean while he assailed the seasons
He wept that he was ever born, And he had reasons.
Miniver loved the days of old When swords were bright and steeds were prancing;
The vision of a warrior bold Would send him dancing.
Miniver sighed for what was not, And dreamed, and rested from his labors;
He dreamed of Thebes and Camelot, And Priam's neighbors.
Miniver mourned the ripe renown That made so many a name so fragrant;
He mourned Romance, now on the town, And Art, a vagrant.
Miniver loved the Medici, Albeit he had never seen one;
He would have sinned incessantly Could he have been one.
Miniver cursed the commonplace And eyed a khaki suit with loathing:
He missed the medieval grace Of iron clothing.

Miniver scorned the gold he sought, But sore annoyed was he without it;
Miniver thought, and thought, and thought, And thought about it.
Miniver Cheevy, born too late, Scratched his head and kept on thinking;
Miniver coughed, and called it fate, And kept on drinking.

The title character in Edwin Arlington Robinson's poem "Miniver Cheevy" is a classic case of someone who believes something other than what they have—or in this case, the time they live—is far more preferable. He dreams of medieval times, romanticizing their "iron clothing" of armor, and the qualities it represented: respect, bravery, honor, and valor. This romanticized idea becomes obsession, intensifying his disdain for and inability to cope in the present. His idealized vision of the medieval period fails to consider its downfalls, such as disease and starvation. The poem also depicts Cheevy's hypocrisy, noting that he "scorned the gold he sought, But sore annoyed was he without it." Ultimately, Cheevy blames his "misfortune" on the fate of being born too late, and chooses to take the escapist route with alcohol. And in a cyclical patter, the alcohol continues to foster his illusion that the grass is greener on the other side.

The Tuft of Flowers

I went to turn the grass once after one Who mowed it in the dew before the sun.
The dew was gone that made his blade so keen Before I came to view the leveled scene.
I looked for him behind an isle of trees; I listened for his whetstone on the breeze.
But he had gone his way, the grass all mown, And I must be, as he had been—alone,
'As all must be,' I said within my heart, 'Whether they work together or apart.'
But as I said it, swift there passed me by On noiseless wing a bewildered butterfly,
Seeking with memories grown dim o'er night Some resting flower of yesterday's delight.
And once I marked his flight go round and round, As where some flower lay withering on the ground.
And then he flew as far as eye could see, And then on tremulous wing came back to me.
I thought of questions that have no reply, And would have turned to toss the grass to dry;
But he turned first, and led my eye to look At a tall tuft of flowers beside a brook,
A leaping tongue of bloom the scythe had spared Beside a reedy brook the scythe had bared.
The mower in the dew had loved them thus, By leaving them to flourish, not for us,
Nor yet to draw one thought of ours to him, But from sheer morning gladness at the brim.
The butterfly and I had lit upon, Nevertheless, a message from the dawn,
That made me hear the wakening birds around, And hear his long scythe whispering to the ground,
And feel a spirit kindred to my own; So that henceforth I worked no more alone;

But glad with him, I worked as with his aid, And weary, sought at noon with him the shade;
And dreaming, as it were, held brotherly speech With one whose thought I had not hoped to reach.
'Men work together,' I told him from the heart, 'Whether they work together or apart.'

In Robert Frost's "The Tuft of Flowers," the speaker is in a field where he intends to turn mowed grass. He feels lonely in his work—not just a sense of being alone, but the profound loneliness that exists in the human condition. He then sights a butterfly, which leads his eyes to a tuft of flowers that the mower left standing. Recognizing that the admiring mower spared the flowers in his duties, a sense of joy is awakened in the speaker. He feels a kinship with the mower, recognizing that their values align. This revelation banishes his loneliness, and just as before he felt the loneliness of the human condition, he now has a feeling of aligned purpose, one that makes him feel as though he and the mower are working side by side.

Sympathy

I know what the caged bird feels, alas!
Ah me, when the sun is bright on the upland slopes,
when the wind blows soft through the springing grass
and the river floats like a sheet of glass,
when the first bird sings and the first bud opes,
and the faint perfume from its chalice steals—
I know what the caged bird feels!

I know why the caged bird beats his wing
till its blood is red on the cruel bars,
for he must fly back to his perch and cling
when he fain would be on the bow a-swing.
And the blood still throbs in the old, old scars
and they pulse again with a keener sting—
I know why he beats his wing!

I know why the caged bird sings, ah me,
When his wing is bruised and his bosom sore,
When he beats his bars and he would be free;
It is not a carol of joy or glee,
But a prayer that it sends from his heart's deep core,
But a plea, that upward to heaven it flings.
I know why the caged bird sings!

The poem "Sympathy," by Paul Laurence Dunbar, suggests to the reader a comparison between the lifestyle of the caged bird, and the African American in the 19th century. He reveals how the African American identifies and relates to the frustrations and pain that a caged bird experiences, understanding what it's like to have freedom just out of reach. The second stanza focuses on the futile efforts of the bird trying desperately to break from his cage. The pain is internal, and the "scars" represent those of slavery, always being reopened during the fight for equality. Scars could also represent the methods used to punish slaves who tried to escape, either beating or lynching. The last stanza illustrates the undaunted hope of the African American. Though "his wing is bruised and his bosom sore" he continues to believe in the possibility of freedom. He prays to the heavens in a plea for divine intervention, singing his prayer that it might be heard.

Bury Me In a Free Land

Make me a grave where'er you will,
In a lowly plain, or a lofty hill;
Make it among earth's humblest graves,
But not in a land where men are slaves.

I could not rest if around my grave
I heard the steps of a trembling slave;
His shadow above my silent tomb
Would make it a place of fearful gloom.

I could not rest if I heard the tread
Of coffle gang to the shambles led,
And the mother's shriek of wild despair
Rise like a curse on the trembling air.

I could not sleep if I saw the lash
Drinking her blood at each fearful gash,
And I saw her babes torn from her breast,
Like trembling doves from their parent
nest.

I'd shudder and start if I heard the bay
Of bloodhounds seizing their human prey,
And I heard the captive plead in vain
As they bound afresh his galling chain.

If I saw young girls from their mother's
arms
Bartered and sold for their youthful
charms,
My eye would flash with a mournful
flame,
My death-paled cheek grow red with
shame.

I would sleep, dear friends, where bloated might
Can rob no man of his dearest right;
My rest shall be calm in any grave
Where none can call his brother a slave.

I ask no monument, proud and high,
To arrest the gaze of the passers-by;
All that my yearning spirit craves,
Is bury me not in a land of slaves.

Straightforward in title and verse, Frances Ellen Watkins Harper's poem, "Bury Me in a Free Land," is at its heart a poem about justice and freedom. In the first stanza, she declares that it matters not where she is buried—whether it is a noble hill or the humblest of graves, as long as the land in which she is buried is free. In the second through sixth stanzas, she names several circumstances that would prevent her from knowing peaceful rest in her grave: a "trembling" slave, a "mother's shriek of wild despair," the lashing of a slave, bloodhounds seizing their prey, and young girls bartered into slavery. In the seventh stanza, she declares that she would only be able to sleep if no man were robbed of his freedom ("his dearest right") and the last stanza re-states that her spirit wants nothing more than to be buried in a land that is free.

Mr. Flood's Party

There was not much that was ahead of him, / And there was nothing in the town below—/ Where strangers would have shut the many doors / That many friends had opened long ago.

"Mr. Flood's Party," by Edwin Arlington Robinson, is a sad portrait of the extremely lonely Eben Flood, who believes he has outlived his usefulness. Although harvested crops still serve a purpose at the end of their cycle, Eben believes his future has no meaning, as he is of no use to anyone at this stage in his life. Hence, "there was not much that was ahead of him." He also felt that the community in which he lived was nothing more than a town of "strangers," who would shut the door at his approach. He reflects that the same doors that would close on him now were opened and welcoming to him "long ago." The poem also reveals that Eben knows there is more to him than meets the townspeople's eyes. They only know the drunken man he has become, and not the young man who possessed an appreciation of poetry. Now he finds refuge in alcohol, as he spends his elderly years without friends or family.

The Stirrup-Cup

Death, thou'rt a cordial old and rare:
Look how compounded, with what care!
Time got his wrinkles reaping thee

Sweet herbs from all antiquity.

David to thy distillage went,
Keats, and Gotama excellent,
Omar Khayyam, and Chaucer bright,
And Shakespeare for a king-delight.

Then, Time, let not a drop be spilt:
Hand me the cup whene'er thou wilt;
'Tis thy rich stirrup-cup to me;
I'll drink it down right smilingly.

In olden days when a man was heading out on a journey, it was customary for one who loved him to bring a glass of wine while he sat in the saddle, feet in the stirrups. It was traditional to use port or sherry, and was referred to in G. G. Coulton's *Chaucer and his England* when the Canterbury pilgrims set out. In Sidney Lanier's "The Stirrup-Cup," however, the cup contains a different concoction—that is, death. The speaker admires the contents of the stirrup-cup, calling it "cordial old and rare," and praising its "sweet herbs from all antiquity." He makes reference to other literary works where the stirrup-cup was used, and finally, addresses time, letting it know that whenever it is his time to drink of death from the cup, the speaker will do so "smilingly."

The House of Mirth

1. ...as though she were a captured dryad subdued to the conventions of the drawing room.

2. I have tried hard—but life is difficult, and I am a very useless person. I can hardly be said to have an independent existence. I was just a screw or a cog in the great machine I called life, and when I dropped out of it I found I was of no use anywhere else.

In Edith Wharton's *The House of Mirth*, Lawrence Selden, Lily Barton's friend and sometime suitor, foreshadows what would eventually be Lily's downfall: a spirit larger than the role society requires of women. His description denotes a kind of "trap" that is Lily's situation, a position that would only be amplified by slander and social rejection of several vicious society women. Lily does not entirely escape the blame for her ever-declining social status. Several times she is on the verge of a good marriage, but sabotages each opportunity, unwilling to play by the rules of society. Rumors of debt, a blatant lie accusing her of adultery, and the social fallout stemming from that lie—including her aunt's decision to disinherit her—lead to Lily working menial jobs to support herself, until she tragically commits suicide, perhaps accidentally, with sleeping pills. Her tragic farewell statement admits fault for her situation, and depicts the cruelty of the social ladder's "survival of the fittest."

The Wayfarer

The wayfarer,
Perceiving the pathway to truth,
Was struck with astonishment.
It was thickly grown with weeds.
"Ha," he said,
"I see that none has passed here
In a long time."
Later he saw that each weed
Was a singular knife.
"Well," he mumbled at last,
"Doubtless there are other roads."

In Stephen Crane's "The Wayfarer," a traveler sets out down the "pathway to truth," a road found to be scarcely traveled. In fact, the traveler is astonished to see that path was so unused, it had become "thickly grown with weeds." The growth of the weeds makes him realize that it has been quite some time since someone else has attempted this same journey. But upon closer analysis, the traveler learns to his probable horror, that each weed was actually a "singular knife." Contemplating this for a moment, he finally concludes that there are other, easier roads than this. Crane does not reveal if the traveler then decides to travel the easier road, or to brave the path of knives, but that is the suggestion, and if the traveler does change course, he will never discover truth.

Solitude

Laugh, and the world laughs with you;
Weep, and you weep alone.
For the sad old earth must borrow its mirth,
But has trouble enough of its own.
Sing, and the hills will answer;
Sigh, it is lost on the air.
The echoes bound to a joyful sound,
But shrink from voicing care.

Rejoice, and men will seek you;
Grieve, and they turn and go.
They want full measure of all your pleasure,
But they do not need your woe.
Be glad, and your friends are many;
Be sad, and you lose them all.
There are none to decline your nectared wine,
But alone you must drink life's gall.

- 44 -

Feast, and your halls are crowded;
Fast, and the world goes by.
Succeed and give, and it helps you live,
But no man can help you die.
There is room in the halls of pleasure
For a long and lordly train,
But one by one we must all file on
Through the narrow aisles of pain.

Ella Wheeler Wilcox's "Solitude" is a poem about human beings' desire to avoid pain and seek happiness. In that endeavor, people tend to avoid the company of those who are suffering, and be in the company of those who are happy. The first stanza reminds the reader that even the earth "must borrow its mirth," meaning that it too only experiences joy by drawing on the joy of others. It cites singing and sighing as examples—the joyful sound of song will be returned as an echo, but the despairing sigh will be "lost on the air." In the second stanza, she reiterates that people gravitate toward those who rejoice, and turn away from those who grieve. Everyone wants to drink "nectared wine," but none wish to share the drink of life's "gall." The third stanza also illustrates this point, reminding readers that the halls of pleasure are big enough for a "large and lordly train," but alas, pain is something we must pass through alone.

The Sea Gypsy

I am fevered with the sunset,
I am fretful with the bay,
For the wander-thirst is on me
And my soul is in Cathay.
There's a schooner in the offing,
With her topsails shot with fire,
And my heart has gone aboard her
For the Islands of Desire.
I must forth again tomorrow!
With the sunset I must be
Hull down on the trail of rapture
In the wonder of the sea.

In Richard Hovey's "The Sea Gypsy," he expresses the intense emotion he feels when looking out to sea and witnessing its beauty. He describes the physical reaction of being "fevered" when looking at the sunset, and "fretful" when looking upon the bay. He dreams of being in a faraway destination, putting his soul in "Cathay," which is northern China. He imagines a sailboat will soon appear, with reflections of the sunset on its sails, and though he stands as an observer, his heart has already "gone aboard her," sailing for "the Islands of Desire." He knows that tomorrow he will be there admiring the same sight, in his desire to experience the "wonder of the sea" at sunset.

If I Should Die

If I should die to-night
And you should come to my cold corpse and say,
Weeping and heartsick o'er my lifeless clay—
If I should die tonight,
And you should come in deepest grief and woe—
And say: "Here's that ten dollars that I owe,"
I might arise in my large white cravat
And say, "What's that?"

If I should die to-night
And you should come to my cold corpse and kneel,
Clasping my bier to show the grief you feel,
I say, if I should die to-night
And you should come to me, and there and then
Just even hint 'bout payin' me that ten,
I might arise the while,
But I'd drop dead again.

Ben King's humorous poem and parody, "If I Should Die," takes a serious matter—death—and combines it with a humorous situation—the debt of ten dollars owed to the deceased. In the first stanza, he suggests a hypothetical situation. "If" he should die tonight, and this debtor came to his corpse weeping and filled with woe, and in despair offered to pay back the ten dollars that he owed, the narrator might just sit up in his coffin and respond, having heard the offer. In the second stanza the grief intensifies as the debtor is kneeling at the corpse, "clasping my bier." Even the suggestion of having the ten dollars returned might prompt him certainly to arise. But ultimately, he is dead, so though the offer would pique his interest, it is simply too late to make good on the debt.

The Daguerreotype

This, then, is she,
My mother as she looked at seventeen,
When she first met my father. Young incredibly,
Younger than spring, without the faintest trace
Of disappointment, weariness, or tean
Upon the childlike earnestness and grace
Of the waiting face.
Those close-wound ropes of pearl
(Or common beads made precious by their use)
Seem heavy for so slight a throat to wear;
But the low bodice leaves the shoulders bare
And half the glad swell of the breast, for news

- 46 -

That now the woman stirs within the girl.
And yet,
Even so, the loops and globes
Of beaten gold
And jet
Hung, in the stately way of old,
From the ears' drooping lobes
On festivals and Lord's-day of the week,
Show all too matron-sober for the
cheek,—
Which, now I look again, is perfect child,
Or no—or no—'t is girlhood's very self,
Moulded by some deep, mischief-ridden elf
So meek, so maiden mild,
But startling the close gazer with the sense
Of passions forest-shy and forest-wild,
And delicate delirious merriments.

"The Daguerreotype," by William Vaughn Moody, is an elegy inspired by a portrait of Moody's mother at the young age of 17. He first notes that it was around the time she met his father, and that she was "younger than spring." Her youth bears no evidence yet of the disappointment and weariness life would surely bring, just a "waiting face," waiting and looking forward to experiencing life. And although her neck seems childlike for the pearls that she wears, the swell of her breasts is evidence that she is no longer a child, but a young woman. He also notes the earrings worn for special occasions, such as festivals or Sundays, and at first glance he sees a "perfect child," but upon second glance sees a combination of meek yet mischievous eyes, a mixture of shy yet wild, delicate yet delirious, as she at 17 is on the verge of womanhood.

Good and Bad Luck

Good luck is the gayest of all gay girls;
Long in one place she will not stay:
Back from your brow she strokes the curls,
Kisses you quick and flies away.
But Madame Bad Luck soberly comes
And stays, —no fancy has she for flitting,—
Snatches of true-love songs she hums,
And sits by your bed, and brings her knitting.

"Good luck" can be defined as an unknown or unpredictable situation or phenomenon that leads to a favorable outcome, while "bad luck" has just the opposite outcome, often leading the unlucky to describe himself a "victim of circumstance." In John Hay's "Good and Bad Luck," he personifies the two. Good luck is a happy-go-lucky girl who brings nothing but fortune and happiness wherever she goes, though she never remains in one place for very long. But while with you, she showers kisses before her rapid departure. Hay ages his personification of luck when he describes "Madame" Bad Luck. Unlike her carefree opposite, who comes and goes in an instant, Madame Bad Luck is the guest that simply won't leave. She comes soberly, she creates a solemn mood, and not only remains in your company but "sits by your bed and brings her knitting." Hay offers no comment on how to make her go, only focusing on the contrast of their arrival and departure.

Columbus

Then, pale and worn, he kept his deck,
And peered through darkness. Ah, that
night
Of all dark nights! And then a speck—
A light! a light! a light! a light!
It grew; a starlit flag unfurled!
It grew to be Time's burst of dawn.
He gained a world; he gave that world
Its grandest lesson: 'On! sail on!'

Composed in 1892, Joaquin Miller's "Columbus" was written in honor of the 400th anniversary of the discovery of America. Though many writings exist for the purpose of dramatizing the initial voyage of Columbus, Miller's poem is more of an encouragement. This final stanza is the climax of a long, hard voyage at which point Columbus is "pale and worn." But though exhausted from his journey, he remained on deck keeping a watchful eye, when finally one night, as he "peered through darkness," he finally saw a speck, which turned out to be a light, signifying land. And as he neared land, the light became bigger and brighter, being as "Time's burst of dawn." This discovery of light was the discovery of a world, and it was all because he chose to continue sailing—"On! Sail on!"

In Men Whom Men Condemn

In men whom men condemn as ill
I find so much of goodness still.
In men whom men pronounce divine
I find so much of sin and blot
I do not dare to draw a line
Between the two, where God has not.

This short poem, "In Men Whom Men Condemn" by Joaquin Miller, uses few words to touch upon a meaningful subject. "In men whom condemn" refers to any man, or woman, who has been condemned for some specific sin or crime by society, whether they are simply a societal outcast, or perhaps imprisoned for a crime. Though condemned, Miller finds that they are not without goodness. Whatever their sin or crime, that does not define the entire person. He then takes a look at men who are considered "divine" by the people, put on a pedestal for their goodness. Just as he finds goodness in men who are condemned, he finds "sin and blot" in those who are highly esteemed. Therefore, he will not dare to stereotype or categorize these men, placing them in separate corners, as God himself does not do this. "Judge not lest ye be judged" is a central theme of this poem.

Little Orphant Annie

Little Orphant Annie's come to our house to stay,
An' wash the cups an' saucers up, an' brush the crumbs away,
An' shoo the chickens off the porch, an' dust the hearth, an' sweep,
An' make the fire, an' bake the bread, an' earn her board-an'-keep;
An' all us other childern, when the supper-things is done,
We set around the kitchen fire an' has the mostest fun
A-list'nin' to the witch-tales 'at Annie tells about,
An' the Gobble-uns 'at gits you Ef you Don't Watch Out!

Wunst they wuz a little boy wouldn't say his prayers,—
An' when he went to bed at night, away up-stairs,
His Mammy heerd him holler, an' his Daddy heerd him bawl,
An' when they turn't the kivvers down, he wuzn't there at all!
An' they seeked him in the rafter-room, an' cubby-hole, an' press,
An' seeked him up the chimbly-flue, an' ever'-wheres, I guess;
But all they ever found wuz thist his pants an' roundabout: —
An' the Gobble-uns 'll git you Ef you Don't Watch Out!

An' one time a little girl 'ud allus laugh an' grin,
An' make fun of ever' one, an' all her blood-an'-kin;
An' wunst, when they was "company," an' ole folks wuz there,
She mocked 'em an' shocked 'em, an' said she didn't care!
An' thist as she kicked her heels, an' turn't to run an' hide,
They wuz two great big Black Things a-standin' by her side,
An' they snatched her through the ceilin' 'fore she knowed what she's about!
An' the Gobble-uns 'll git you Ef you Don't Watch Out!

An' little Orphant Annie says, when the blaze is blue,
An' the lamp-wick sputters, an' the wind goes woo-oo!
An' you hear the crickets quit, an' the moon is gray,
An' the lightnin'-bugs in dew is all squenched away, —
You better mind yer parunts, an' yer teachurs fond an' dear,
An' churish them 'at loves you, an' dry the orphant's tear,
An' he'p the pore an' needy ones 'at clusters all about,
Er the Gobble-uns 'll git you Ef you Don't Watch Out!

The Little Orphan Annie that Riley is writing about was a real person: Mary Alice Smith, an orphan who came to live in the Riley home in return for doing chores around the house. Mary Alice had a big imagination, and used to tell tall tales. This poem depicts those tales she told as the other family members sat around the fire. The first is about a little boy who wouldn't say his prayers. One night his mother and father responded to his screams and cries, but found only his pants and no trace of him. The second tale is about a mean-hearted girl who mocks others' families, only to be snatched through the ceiling by two "great big Black Things." Then she warns that if they don't want this to happen to them, they better listen to their parents, teachers, and loved ones, help the poor, needy and orphaned, "Er the Gobble-uns'll git you Ef you Don't Watch Out!"

Little Boy Blue

The little toy dog is covered with dust,
But sturdy and stanch he stands;
And the little toy soldier is red with rust,
And his musket moulds in his hands.
Time was when the little toy dog was new,
And the soldier was passing fair;
And that was the time when our Little Boy Blue
Kissed them and put them there.
"Now, don't you go till I come," he said,
"And don't you make any noise!"
So, toddling off to his trundle-bed,
He dreamt of the pretty toys;
And, as he was dreaming, an angel song
Awakened our Little Boy Blue—
Oh! the years are many, the years are long,
But the little toy friends are true!
Ay, faithful to Little Boy Blue they stand,
Each in the same old place—
Awaiting the touch of a little hand,
The smile of a little face;
And they wonder, as waiting the long years through
In the dust of that little chair,
What has become of our Little Boy Blue,
Since he kissed them and put them there.

"Little Boy Blue," by Eugene Field, begins with a description of two toys that belong to a little boy: a toy dog and toy soldier. Once loved and played with, the toys now sit covered with dust, where the boy last kissed them and placed them. The boy instructs the toys not to go anywhere or make any noise as he goes to bed, where he dreams of them. But he is awakened by an angel song that calls him to heaven. Now so many years later, his "friends" remain just as he left them, loyal and true. They wonder where he is, as they sit there waiting for "the touch of a little hand, the smile of a little face." It is widely known now that this much-loved poem was written about the author's own son, who died when he was just a young boy.

Historical and Social Settings

Daisy Miller

Henry James's *Daisy Miller* portrays the courtship of title character, a beautiful American girl, by the sophisticated European, Winterbourne. Winterbourne frowns on Daisy's natural flirtatiousness, and he is surrounded by friends and relatives who disapprove of the pairing, believing Daisy to be shameless and common. As tensions build, and Daisy remains undeterred, Winterbourne tells himself Daisy is too common for him to love. He warns her about "Roman fever" and she rushes home, only to die a few days later. This story provides an analysis of traditional views that label others as outsiders. Henry James uses Daisy's story to discuss what he thinks Europeans and Americans believed about each other at this time, which can also apply to the prejudices common in any culture.

Uncle Remus

The "Uncle Remus" stories, by Joel Chandler Harris, were revolutionary in their use of dialect, written exactly as spoken by the characters. For example, the name of one of the main characters is Br'er Rabbit, which means "Brother" Rabbit. Published in 1876, Harris's stories focus on the post-American Civil War period, when slavery and white supremacy were reigning issues in America. Uncle Remus is the narrator, and the animals in the stories represent the white and black populations and the tensions between the races. A common theme in Uncle Remus's stories was triumph that resulted not from physical strength but intellectual prowess. Through humorous and adventurous depictions, Harris provided a series of stories rich with lessons on social order and how we treat our fellow man.

The Revolt of 'Mother'

"The Revolt of 'Mother,'" by Mary E. Wilkins Freeman, is set in the late 1800s, during a time when women were perceived as being inferior to men. In the story, the characterization of "Mother" is that of a meek woman, described as having a "forehead mild and benevolent ..." with "meek downward lines about her nose and mouth." Thus, meek, mild, and benevolent were the traits of women of that time period. In "The Revolt of 'Mother,'" Freeman conveys women's lack of power, but also demonstrates that she and all women can stand up for themselves and make a difference. This depiction provides understanding of a time when women were thought to be weaker, less intelligent, and less important than men, while also breaking ground to reveal how to get around such inequality.

The Passing of Grandison

"Slave narrative" generally refers to the autobiographical works of ex-slaves, documenting their experiences and usually their escape from slavery. Like most slave narratives, "The Passing of Grandison," by Charles W. Chesnutt, records the circumstances defining the lives of slaves on a southern plantation, the travails of a particular slave—in this case, Grandison, and his own eventual escape to the North with his family. It also refers to Grandison's use of the North Star as a navigational tool, another element characteristic in slave narratives. However, "The Passing of Grandison" differs from the traditional slave narrative in that it is much shorter than the typical book-length narrative, and far less predictable. Other authors of slave narrative include Frederick Douglass, Solomon Northrup, and Harriet Jacobs.

John Lamar and Life in the Iron Mills

Rebecca Harding Davis, whose works serve as classic examples of American realism, is known for her passionate writings that at times harbor naturalistic sentiments. In "John Lamar," set during the American Civil war, Davis condemns slavery and those who misuse the Bible to justify the brutality of their actions. "Life in the Iron Mills" highlights the hell experienced by the 19th-century immigrant workers who were exploited and poorly educated. This story also reveals that the Bible is quoted by the tormentors to justify their exploitation and cruelty. Davis's tales were often concerned with pressing issues of her era—preceding William Dean Howells's "theory of the commonplace" by over 20 years. Additionally, her portrayal of the psychological torment of American Civil War soldiers preceded that of Stephen Crane's by many years, and her study of the social imprisonment of Victorian women preceded Kate Chopin's.

Literary Devices

To Build a Fire

Three naturalistic elements that appear in Jack London's "To Build a Fire" are: its narrative form, its theme of an indifferent environment, and its strong focus on processes. London provides the reader with a virtually non-stop narrative drive, which keeps the story plot-driven as opposed to character-driven. London does not give the main character a name, indicating how little he is concerned with him as a unique person. Naturalism also maintains that the environment is indifferent. In "To Build a Fire," the reader sees indifference in the bitter cold of the Yukon. Despite the main character's struggle to survive, the weather remains bitterly cold in this story of man versus nature. Thirdly, the story places a strong focus on processes, another common element of naturalism. It provides a detailed description of building a fire, and reveals that, while the main character is adept with physical processes, his failure to consider potential consequences and link together crucial mental processes was ultimately his downfall.

Richard Cory

Whenever Richard Cory went down town,
We people on the pavement looked at him:
He was a gentleman from head to crown,
Clean favored, and imperially slim.

And he was always quietly arrayed,
And he was always human when he
talked;
But he still fluttered pulses when he said,
"Good-morning," and he glittered when
he walked.
And he was rich—yes, richer than a king—
and admirably schooled in every grace:
In fine, we thought that he was everything
To make us wish that we were in his place.
So on we worked, and waited for the light, And went without the meat, and cursed
the bread;
And Richard Cory, one calm summer night,
Went home and put a bullet through his head.

The verse form of Edwin Arlington Robinson's "Richard Cory" is simple and classic.
Though this form is considered old for its time, rigid, and formulated, the personal
subject matter and modern subject make it highly intriguing both in its time and in
present day. The rhyme scheme is the classic iambic pentameter with an ABAB,
CDCD, EFEF, GHGH pattern. The lines are dived into four stanzas, called quatrains,
and the meter is also simple and classic. This classic style is much more reminiscent
of English predecessors William Shakespeare, Ben Johnson and John Milton, in
contrast to the more popular free form of Robinson's day, as seen in the works of
Walt Whitman, Henry David Thoreau and Wallace Stevens.

Modernism (1910–1945)

The Sound and the Fury

William Faulkner's *The Sound and the Fury* depicts the decline of the Compson
family, a once noble Southern family descended from U.S. Civil War hero General
Compson. Told from different perspectives of various characters, the reader learns
how the family falls victim to those vices that were problematic in the reconstructed
South: racism, avarice and selfishness. Over several decades, the reader learns how
the family falls into financial ruin and loses its religious faith and the respect of the
town of Jefferson. Many within the Compson family die tragically. Faulkner tells the
story in four parts: first from the perspective of Benjy Compson, an intellectually

disabled man; the second from the viewpoint of Quentin Compson, set 18 years earlier than the other three sections; the third from the point of view of Jason, the embittered brother; and the fourth from a third-person point of view focused on Dilsey, the Compson family's black servant.

Of Mice and Men

Set in California during the Great Depression, John Steinbeck's *Of Mice and Men* tells the story of two migrant field workers, George Milton and Lennie Small, who share a dream of settling down on their own piece of land. George is an intelligent yet cynical man, and Lennie is a large, strong man, but has limited mental abilities. Lennie delights in hearing about the day he will tend to the land they own and stroke soft rabbits. On a ranch where George and Lennie work, their dream begins to come within reach. But when Lennie innocently tries to stroke the hair of the ranch owner's daughter-in-law, he accidentally kills her. Wishing to spare Lennie from the lynch mob searching for him, George shoots him in the back of the head. Powerlessness is a central theme throughout. Lennie is physically strong but his intellectual handicap renders him powerless in his demise. George, Lennie, Candy and Crooks endure economic powerlessness, as they are unable to generate enough money to purchase a homestead.

Great Gatsby

Characters from F. Scott Fitzgerald's *The Great Gatsby*
- Nick Carraway
- Daisy Buchanan
- Tom Buchanan
- Jay Gatsby
- Jordan Baker

In F. Scott Fitzgerald's *The Great Gatsby*, narrator Nick Carraway, originally from Minnesota, is the Long Island neighbor of Gatsby, a Yale graduate, a World War I, and works as a bond salesman. Daisy Buchanan is Nick's second cousin once removed, an attractive young woman married to Tom Buchanan. Before marriage, she was courted by Jay Gatsby, but the relationship ended due to their different social standings. Tom Buchanan is an arrogant "old money" millionaire, and also a Yale graduate. Originally from North Dakota, Jay Gatsby is a young, mysterious self-made millionaire with shady business connections, who remains in love with Daisy Buchanan. Jordan Baker is Daisy Buchanan's long-time friend, and a professional golf player with a slightly shady reputation.

One of Ours

In Willa Cather's *One of Ours*, Claude Wheeler is an idealistic and sensitive young man trapped in a life that he feels is lacking, but unsure what it is he hopes to find.

Forced to give up his schooling to help his family's farm business, he enters a marriage with a wife who places all of her focus on missionary work. Claude is a dreamer with a sense of having a greater purpose, but is held back by an increasingly hopeless situation. But it is then that America enters World War I, and Claude discovers his destiny during a journey that will prove to be his last. It is the picture of innocence and then innocence lost in the midst of death, suffering and the horrors of war that provides the intense emotional impact of this story. Claude gets to see the world and meet others to whom he can relate, but ironically, the war that made him feel alive ultimately takes his life at a young age.

My Antonia

Characters in Willa Cather's *My Antonia*

My Antonia, by Willa Cather, is a novel about several immigrant families who move to Black Hawk, Nebraska. From Bohemia, Antonia is the free-hearted eldest daughter of the Shimerdas. Soon after their move, her father commits suicide as a result of his depression of having to leave the old country. Antonia endures a difficult period of farming after her father dies, and suffers several hardships, including being left by her fiancé Larry Donovan while pregnant with his child. She later marries a man named Cuzak, and they have ten children on the farm. Jim Burden is the narrator of the novel and Antonia's childhood friend in Nebraska. Although he becomes romantically interested in her, he learns that Antonia, who is four years his senior, thinks of him as a child. Jim eventually attends Harvard Law School in Boston, but returns to Black Hawk after 20 years and finds Antonia and her new family. He reflects in the closing lines of the book that "we possessed together the precious, the incommunicable past."

A Farewell to Arms

Ernest Hemingway's *A Farewell to Arms* has many images of nature that recur throughout the work, particularly in the first chapter. Two of the most prominent symbols are rain and mud. Virtually every time something bad occurs, such as the army's retreat or Catherine's death, it is raining outside. The rain serves to mark these events as random occurrences, much like rain itself. But rain also serves as a life-affirming symbol. It rains when Henry decides to desert the Italian army. Representing death at times and affirmation of life at others, Hemingway reveals that like nature, control over blessings and curses is not within the hands of man. Mud is another recurring symbol in *A Farewell to Arms*, serving as an obstacle to the army both in offense and retreat, demonstrating nature's hostility toward man.

The Hairy Ape

The Hairy Ape, by Eugene O'Neill, is about a man named Richard "Yank" Smith, an apelike coal stoker on a luxury liner. When Mildred Douglas, the daughter of the liner's president, visits the boiler room, she faints at the sight of the man's brutish appearance. A powerhouse of a man with a primitive confidence, Hank has never been looked down on before nor suffered the insult "hairy ape," flung at him by the rich girl. Taken aback by her behavior, Yank begins to question his worth and his place in society. He leaves the ship to stroll up Fifth Avenue, where his boorish behavior lands him in jail. Cell mates urge him to join the "Wobblies," but the union refuses him. Confused and upset, he heads for a zoo and asks a gorilla "Where do I fit in?" He attempts to release the animal, but the gorilla, too, misunderstands him and kills him. *The Hairy Ape* is a strong condemnation of the dehumanizing effects of industrialization.

The Love Song of J. Alfred Prufrock

"The Love Song of J. Alfred Prufrock," by T. S. Eliot, is a dramatic monologue spoken by J. Alfred Prufrock, a balding, insecure, middle-aged man who expresses feelings of inadequacy, fear of making decisions, and his many thoughts about the mediocre life he leads as a result of these insecurities. Though he would like to and occasionally attempts to make progress in his life, fear of failure and a timid nature prevent him from seeing it through. Because Prufrock has numerous anxieties, resists making decisions, and focuses intently on the negatives of his life, as well as other people's lives, three themes central to the poem are alienation, indecision, and pessimism. Thus, "The Love Song of J. Alfred Prufrock" is a depiction of loneliness in this ironically titled monologue.

The Book of the Grotesque

"The Book of the Grotesque," the prologue to Sherwood Anderson's book of short stories *Winesburg, Ohio*, tells the tale of an old writer who hires a carpenter to raise his bed so he can see out of his window, but spends most of the time exchanging stories with him about the Civil War. In bed, the writer notices a fluttering in his heart and begins to contemplate death. From this contemplation, he feels young, like there is a young woman inside of him, and from this young woman originates a stream of people he has known throughout his life. The writer begins writing down "truths," from poverty to passion, and assigns one or more truths to the "characters" in his life. Thus, they transform into a "grotesque," in which the truth they embrace becomes a falsehood. The old carpenter who fixed his bed became "the nearest thing to what is understandable and lovable of all the grotesques in the writer's book."

The Curious Case of Benjamin Button

"The Curious Case of Benjamin Button" begins with a nameless first-person narrator who has a remarkable tale to share. Benjamin Button was born in the summer of 1860, and to his parents' dismay, this "baby" is actually a 70-year-old man. Benjamin ages in reverse, getting younger at the same rate that everyone else gets older. When Benjamin appears 50, but has actually been alive only 20 years, he meets and falls in love with the beautiful young Hildegarde Moncrief. They marry and have a son, Roscoe, but as Hildegarde gets older, Benjamin gets younger, and loses interest in his wife. He fights in the Spanish-American War, getting younger every year, and returns close to the same age as his son. He enrolls in Harvard at about age 18, and eventually grows young enough to play together as children with his grandson. Finally, Benjamin is a baby and forgets everything he's done in his life, until his basic infant sensations fade to darkness.

The Chrysanthemums

Elisa Allen and her husband Henry live on their peaceful farm in the Salinas Valley. One day while Elisa is busy tending to her garden, a tinker passes by their farm. Stating he is in need of work, he asks to fix some cutlery and pans. At first Elisa resists, but he shows an interest in her prized chrysanthemums and asks for some shoots to take to a lady who had once asked for some. Elisa is happy to offer him some shoots and explains in great detail how to care for them. She then allows him to fix some old dented pans, even though she is capable of doing it herself, as he claims to have no money. Later, Elisa and Henry are in their car on the way to town, she sees the chrysanthemum shoots she had given him thrown carelessly on the road, but noticed he had kept the pot. Elisa is deeply hurt by this, realizing he had lied just to flatter her and get some business.

Spotted Horses

William Faulkner's *Spotted Horses* deals with the same family introduced in "Bar Burning," the Snopeses. In *Spotted Horses*, born con man Flem Snopes launches a scheme to auction off a lot of unbroken horses. Henry Armstid, fascinated with the wild creatures, is duped into giving them four dollars, the last money his family has, raised by his wife. Of course, when Armstid tries to collect his horse, he cannot even get a rope around its neck. The horse gets out and runs free, breaking Armstid's legs in the process. Unable to successfully sue for her money back, Mrs. Armstid's long-suffering dignity adds poignancy to the story. This comedy serves a satirical purpose of demonstrating, through Flem Snopes, the rise of "Snopesism," invading the innocence of Yoknapatawpha County with scams and swindling.

The Short Happy Life of Francis Macomber

"The Short Happy Life of Francis Macomber," by Ernest Hemingway, is titled such because very soon after the main character, Francis Macomber, discovers a confident side of himself he had never known, he is killed. Francis and his beautiful but cold-hearted wife, Margot, are on a safari with professional hunter Robert Wilson. The story soon reveals an embarrassing moment in Macomber's hunt, when he runs away from the lion they were hunting. This act of cowardice earns the disgust of his wife, who blatantly sleeps with Wilson following the event. After a night of contemplating why he acted so cowardly, his rocky relationship with his wife, and her betrayal, Macomber engages in the next day's hunt as a newly invigorated man, full of courage, successfully killing two buffalo and wounding one with surprising bravery. However, as the wounded buffalo approaches, Margot shoots Macomber in the back of the head. It is clear she feels threatened by his new sense of self. What isn't clear is whether she killed him intentionally.

Look Homeward, Angel: A Story of the Buried Life

The first part of Thomas Wolfe's *Look Homeward, Angel: A Story of the Buried Life* details the lives of Eugene Gant's mother and father, Eliza and Oliver. After his first marriage ends in tragedy, Oliver becomes an alcoholic. He eventually remarries to Eliza, and they, too, experience a great deal of tragedy, losing several children to illness or in childbirth. But they remain together and have six children. Oliver continues to battle with alcohol, but he is the family's source of strength, forming an especially close bond with Eugene. A reader of Shakespeare, he teaches his daughter Helen to read poetry. And though his relationship with his wife continues to deteriorate due to her increasing impatience with his drinking, through his gusto, Oliver manages to remain the family's primary source of strength and energy.

The Jilting of Granny Weatherall

In Katherine Anne Porter's "The Jilting of Granny Weatherall," Granny Weatherall lies on her bed on what will be her last day. Now 80 years old, her memory takes her back 60 years to the day of her wedding, when the groom left her standing at the altar. The memory of his absence on that day, the wasting of the wedding cake, and the feeling that the walls were falling down all around her is so powerful, she still recalls it with much pain many decades later. As death draws nearer, she is aware of her children hovering over her, and the priest granting her last rites. She realizes she is dying but is taken by surprise and resists. She asks God for a sign reassuring her about the afterlife, but receives nothing, just the surprising feeling of death. She realizes her "bridegroom" has jilted her yet again, making the first jilting seem insignificant in comparison. She swears to never forget being jilted, and with her last breath, blows out the light.

Hills Like White Elephants

"Hills Like White Elephants," by Ernest Hemingway, follows the conversation of a man, referred to only as "the American" and his female companion, Jig. As they sit at a train station in Spain, they drink beer and liquor and discuss an operation the American is attempting to convince Jig to undergo. The reader learns that Jig is pregnant, and though not explicit in the text, the carefully chosen words indicate that the procedure in question is an abortion. Jig's innocence is revealed in her simple observation that the hills across the landscape look like white elephants. White elephant is used to describe a financially burdensome possession, or a possession that is simply unwanted. Though Jig, weary and bored with her traveling lifestyle, may view her pregnancy as an unexpected gift, the American clearly sees the baby as a white elephant—a costly obstacle.

Babylon Revisited

F. Scott Fitzgerald's "Babylon Revisited" is about an alcoholic who has returned to Paris to get custody of his daughter, Honoria, from his late wife's sister, Marion, who was given guardianship several years before. Upon returning to a city where his social circle drank freely and spent freely, he recalls those days that make his current, sober life seem very glum. But determined to regain custody of Honoria, he puts all of his effort into rising above his past. Unfortunately, a couple from that past drunkenly intrudes on dinner with Marion and Honoria one night, an event that leads to his being denied custody. Though he limits himself to one drink a day, the story ends with Charlie sitting in a bar with an empty glass, refusing a refill, for now. The story shows how difficult it is to break away from an addictive cycle, particularly when you place yourself in the same setting that fostered that addiction.

The Second Choice

Theodore Dreiser's "The Second Choice" is told completely from the perspective of a woman. Shirley is reading a farewell letter from Arthur, a smooth-talking, egocentric man with whom she had an affair. Unlike her former, common fiancé Barton, Arthur transformed her drab life. Now learning from his letter that he has moved on, Shirley decides it is necessary to return to Barton, her second choice, and eke out an existence much like that of her parents. She consoles herself with the idea that she will finally realize her dream of standing at the altar in a "pearl satin wedding dress," and she can conjure images of Arthur at will when she needs to recall that exciting time in her life.

Silent Snow, Secret Snow

Conrad Aiken's "Silent Snow, Secret Snow" depicts the sad story of a 12-year-old boy's descent into madness. Sitting in his sixth-grade class, Paul begins daydreaming about snow, and how it muffles the approaching steps of the postman. Even though no snow has actually fallen, Paul's fixation turns into his own reality, in which he begins to believe it is a "secret snow" that nobody else can see. He begins to withdraw more and more from his family and world around him, as he finds this dream world of snow preferable to the "dirty" world. Though his alarmed parents call in a physician, he only responds by becoming increasingly hostile. The story depicts a boy's rejection of reality and a preference for his own private world. Psychoanalysis suggests this is a story about schizophrenia or Asperger syndrome.

U.S.A Trilogy

The *U.S.A. Trilogy*, by John Dos Passos, is comprised of three novels, *The 42nd Parallel*, *1919* and *The Big Money*. This trilogy incorporates four different narrative modes: fictional narratives; collages of newspaper clippings and song lyrics; individually labeled short biographies of current public figures; and fragments of an autobiographical stream of consciousness. The trilogy covers the historical

- 59 -

development of American society during the first three decades of the 20th century, relating the lives of 12 different characters struggling to find their place in society. Though their lives are separate, occasionally the characters interact with one another, while minor characters repeatedly crop up, forming a bridge between the main characters.

Barn Burning

William Faulkner's "Barn Burning" is about ten-year-old Colonel Sartoris "Sarty" Snopes, the son of itinerant farmers. The family has to move around constantly because Sarty's father, Abner Snopes, unleashes his anger against post-Civil War aristocracy by burning down barns. The story centers around the choice with which Sarty is faced: to choose family by defending his father, or morality by exposing his actions. In the past, Abner would warn people that he was about to set a barn ablaze, but he violates this pattern when he plans to burn down the beautiful plantation of the De Spains. Sarty warns them, and thus cuts himself off from his family forever. Having already felt the social isolation resulting from his father's misdeeds, Sarty decides that the only path for him is one that leads away from "the old blood which he had not been permitted to choose for himself."

Blood-Burning Moon

Blood-Burning Moon, by Jean Toomer, opens with Louisa, a black woman who works as a servant for the Stones, as she walks home from work thinking about the two men who are in love with her: Bob Stone and Tom Burwell. Bob is the younger son of her white employers, and Tom is a field worker. She arrives home and sits on the front step still thinking of the men and trying to decide which one she should commit to. She is leaning toward Bob, believing that he can help her escape her life of poverty. When the two men discover they are competing for Louisa, they challenge each other to a fight, and Bob confronts Tom with a knife. Tom slashes Bob's throat, who stumbles home to tell those in his "white" town what happened. A mob quickly forms to lynch Tom. The theme focuses on the quick and intense emergence of racism through love and passion.

Tradition and the Individual Talent

"Tradition and the Individual Talent," by T. S. Eliot, presents Eliot's point of view on the important role tradition plays in poetry, and the direct relationship between the two. Eliot believes that while English tradition recognizes that art progresses through change, or non-tradition, literary advancements are recognized only when they conform to tradition. Eliot saw the past as an important literary component, as we are influenced by the past, and our present relates to the past. He believed that a poet should have knowledge about tradition, since representing traditional ideas and morals are a critical part of poetry. Ironically, Eliot does not mention talent once, despite the essay's title, "Tradition and the Individual Talent," perhaps because he believed talent resulted from a poet's ability to connect with tradition.

He also believed that the ability to do this would inspire novelty, as novelty and progression in literature were directly connected to tapping into tradition.

Death in the Woods

"Death in the Woods," by Sherwood Anderson, is narrated by a witness to an event who is inherently unreliable. Not only did this witness only see part of what occurred, but his subsequent experiences have blurred the lines of reality and illusion. As a boy, the narrator was a partial witness to the death of Ma Grims, an old farm woman who froze to death in the snowy woods when returning from town. Present when her naked body is found, the narrator does not see a deceased old woman, but a figure of romance—a lovely, frozen woman metaphysically transfigured. This "epiphany" becomes as equally important as the parallel perspectives that form the story, addressing the question of perception, and the difficulty in finding authentic truth in memorable events.

Roman Fever

Edith Wharton's "Roman Fever" is the story of two middle-aged American women reflecting on their friendship from the terrace of a restaurant overlooking the sites of Rome. In many ways they have lived parallel lives: they met as young ladies vacationing in Rome, have lived across the street from each other in New York for most of their adult lives, were widowed around the same time, and each has a daughter approximately the same age. But secretly, Mrs. Slade, a self-serving former socialite, has never truly liked Mrs. Ansley. She not only finds her boring, but feels it is unfair that she has a vibrant, adventurous daughter, while her own daughter is boring and reliable. When engaged, she believed Mrs. Ansley was interested in her fiancé, so she set up a meeting between the two as a practical joke. However, that meeting led to the conception of Mrs. Ansley's vivacious daughter, a fact ironically missed while Mrs. Slade focused on the "shortcomings" of her friend.

Poems and Prose

Mending Wall

And on a day we meet to walk the line
And set the wall between us once again.
We keep the wall between us as we go.
To each the boulders that have fallen to each.
And some are loaves and some so nearly balls
We have to use a spell to make them balance:
'Stay where you are until our backs are turned!'
We wear our fingers rough with handling them.
Oh, just another kind of out-door game,
One on a side. It comes to little more:

There where it is we do not need the wall:
He is all pine and I am apple orchard.
My apple trees will never get across
And eat the cones under his pines, I tell him.
He only says, 'Good fences make good neighbors.'

In Robert Frost's "The Mending Wall," the central theme asks the question, is it wise to erect walls and other types of barriers? In this excerpt, although the speaker sees walls as only obstacles to progress and social opportunities, he still assists his neighbor in repairing a wall. They work diligently together for the purpose of putting up a wall between them, an irony that does not go unnoticed by the amused speaker. He light-heartedly tells his neighbor that the pine cones on his trees will now be safe from being eaten by his apple trees. The neighbor, who sees the necessity of fences, replies only, "Good fences make good neighbors." The poem asks the reader to consider both points of view and determine whether fences are necessary never, sometimes or always.

The Seafarer

Lest man know not/That he on dry land loveliest liveth,
List how I, care-wretched, on ice-cold sea,/Weathered the winter, wretched outcast
Deprived of my kinsmen;/Hung with hard ice-flakes, where hail-scur flew,
There I heard naught save the harsh sea/And ice-cold wave, at whiles the swan cries,
Did for my games the gannet's clamour,/Sea-fowls, loudness was for me laughter,
The mews' singing all my mead-drink.
Storms, on the stone-cliffs beaten, fell on the stern/In icy feathers; full oft the eagle screamed
With spray on his pinion.
Not any protector/May make merry man faring needy.
This he little believes, who aye in winsome life/Abides 'mid burghers some heavy business,
Wealthy and wine-flushed, how I weary oft/Must bide above brine.
Days little durable,/And all arrogance of earthen riches,
There come now no kings nor Cæsars/Nor gold-giving lords like those gone.
Howe'er in mirth most magnified,/Whoe'er lived in life most lordliest,
Drear all this excellence, delights undurable!

Ezra Pound's "The Seafarer" is told from the perspective of an old seafarer, who is reminiscing about and evaluating his life. In the first excerpt, he describes the hardships of life on the wintry sea and feelings of anxiousness, hunger, cold wetness and solitude. He contrasts this to life on land, which is free from dangers and filled with food and wine. Though this poem begins as a narrative of a man's life at sea, it becomes a praise of God in the second excerpt. Here the seafarer shifts from the subject of the sea, and focuses on the pathway to heaven. Just as he states the pleasures of living on land, and the contrast to life on the icy sea, he asserts that

- 62 -

earthly happiness does not endure, that "undurable" delights come only to those who live a godly life, not an easy one. He reminds his readers that earthly wealth cannot travel to the afterlife, nor does it determine the wealth of the soul.

What Lips My Lips Have Kissed, and Where and Why

What lips my lips have kissed, and where, and why, /I have forgotten, and what arms have lain
Under my head till morning; but the rain/Is full of ghosts tonight, that tap and sigh
Upon the glass and listen for reply,/And in my heart there stirs a quiet pain
For unremembered lads that not again/Will turn to me at midnight with a cry.
Thus in winter stands the lonely tree, /Nor knows what birds have vanished one by one,
Yet knows its boughs more silent than before:/I cannot say what loves have come and gone,
I only know that summer sang in me/A little while, that in me sings no more.

"What Lips My Lips Have Kissed, and Where, and Why" by Edna St. Vincent Millay laments the loss of lovers from her past. As she tries to recall specifics, she admits, "I cannot say what loves have come and gone," either because too much time has gone by, or she had too many lovers to remember each one. The feeling that she most expresses is loss, and Millay uses comparison images from nature to emphasize her sadness. "Thus in winter stands the lonely tree, Nor knows what birds have vanished one by one, yet knows it boughs more silent than before." She compares herself to a lonely tree, and the birds that have left represent her lovers. And though the tree does not individually recognize each bird, the collective absence and the ensuing silence have brought her to this "winter" season in her life. This sonnet expresses lonesomeness and loss that, unlike the lonely tree, might have been prevented had she not so easily let her lovers fly away.

A Pact

I make a pact with you, Walt Whitman—
I have detested you long enough.
I come to you as a grown child
Who has had a pig-headed father;
I am old enough now to make friends.
It was you that broke the new wood
Now is a time for carving.
We have one sap and one root—
Let there be commerce between us.

"A Pact," by Ezra Pound is the poet's confrontation with Walt Whitman, "a pig-headed father" from the era of Realism and Naturalism, and Pound the grown child in the era of Modernism. Through the confrontation, he is able to express his frustration and acknowledge his debt to his American forebear, the father of free verse expressionism. Though he comes close to being a "grown child" on the verge of a temper tantrum, he stops and turns in another direction, stating that he is old enough now to make friends. In other words, he does not have to live merely in the shadow of his "father," but can take the "new wood" broken by Whitman and with it, create something new—the future of poetry. That link of the new wood and the creation it becomes creates a bond, a pact, that will not give way to vengeance.

The Fish

wade through black jade. Of the crow-blue mussel-shells, one keeps
 adjusting the ash-heaps; opening and shutting itself like
an injured fan. The barnacles which encrust the side
 of the wave, cannot hide there for the submerged shafts of the
sun, split like spun glass, move themselves with spotlight swiftness
into the crevices—in and out, illuminating
the turquoise sea of bodies. The water drives a wedge
 of iron throught the iron edge of the cliff; whereupon the stars,
pink rice-grains, ink-bespattered jelly fish, crabs like green
lilies, and submarine toadstools, slide each on the other.
All external marks of abuse are present on this
defiant edifice—all the physical features of
accident—lack of cornice, dynamite grooves, burns, and
hatchet strokes, these things stand out on it; the chasm-side is
dead. Repeated evidence has proved that it can live
 on what cannot revive its youth. The sea grows old in it.

Ironically, Marianne Moore's poem "The Fish" is not about fish at all. Instead, it focuses on sea life, a seaside cliff, and the sea itself. Like a wave, the poem moves toward one subject then retreats. She describes how the mussels of the sea, though they cling by the side, cannot hide from the "spun-glass" effect of the sun, which illuminates every crevice of every living thing within the sea. She describes the "iron edge" of a seaside cliff, and though the wave is merely water, the ceaseless crashing against the cliff's edge has an equally iron impact, making an opening where living and non-living seep inside, "sliding on each other." It bears the evidence of many years of "abuse," and though it will never be young again, it can live on while the creatures of the sea grow old within it and eventually die. Moore suggests an unresolved paradox—a sea that is abundant yet stark, and the necessary processes of life and death that are part of all natural landscapes.

Historical and Social Settings

The Red Wheelbarrow

so much depends
upon

a red wheel
barrow

glazed with rain
water

beside the white
chickens.

In William Carlos Williams's "The Red Wheel Barrow," lines one and two set the poem's tone. "so much depends upon," a red wheel barrow, as its image is essentially the poem, just as an object within a painting becomes the actual piece of art. After introducing this idea, Williams breaks up the word wheelbarrow, placing "wheel" in line three and "barrow" in line four, to emphasize its basic parts. Breaking it up allows the reader to focus on each part of the object that much more closely. In lines five and six, Williams takes the image of the wheelbarrow that is now embedded in the reader's mind and adds rainwater to it, transforming it from just a red wheelbarrow to one that is "glazed" with rainwater. The final brushstroke of this picture comes in lines seven and eight, when he adds "white" to the imagery, contrasting with red. Now an ordinary wheelbarrow is given an unusual view, glazed with rainwater and in stark contrast to the white chickens. An ordinary sentence becomes poetry with carefully selected imagery and unusual stanza breaks.

My Father's Song

Wanting to say things,/I miss my father tonight.
His voice, the slight catch,/the depth from his thin chest,
the tremble of emotion/in something he has just said/to his son, his <u>song</u>:
We planted corn one Spring at Acu—/we planted several times
But this one particular time/I remember the soft damp sand/in my hand.

My father had stopped at one point/to show me an overturned furrow;
the plowshare had unearthed/the burrow nest of a mouse/in the soft moist sand.
Very gently, he scooped tiny pink animals/into the palm of his hand
and told me to touch them./We took them to the edge
of the field and put them in the shade/of a sand moist clod.

I remember the very softness/of cool and warm sand and tiny alive mice
and my father saying things.

In Simon Ortiz's "My Father's Song," the poem begins with an indication that the
speaker misses his father because he has things he wishes to say to him. But in fact,
we learn that it is his father's voice, and the things he used to hear, that he is truly
missing. He remembers details of his father's voice and the image of his chest,
inflections that indelibly placed the memory of his father's voice on his heart and in
his mind. Of significance are the chosen words, "son" and "song," which have a
closeness in sound and sight that indicates he is his father's "song" by being his
father's "son." Through oral storytelling of small but memorable events, the reader
gets insight into a tradition in which Native Americans not only speak and listen to
one another, but live the process. "My Father's Song" embodies this philosophy,
while readers are made aware of how this method of communication left an
impermeable impression in the mind of the speaker.

Fog

The fog comes
on little cat feet.
It sits looking
over harbor and city
on silent haunches
and then moves on.

Though a mere six lines long, Carl Sandburg's poem "Fog" is an innocent yet deep
expression of finding beauty in an ordinary world. Just as "little cat feet" are silent,
fog creeps toward its destination without warning, arriving quickly yet completely
as it covers a city or harbor. Just as a cat that does as it pleases, fog obeys no rules,
often blocking out all light and making it difficult for others to see. Indifferent to the
quiet nuisance it creates, fog finds its resting place and hovers in that spot, taking in
its surroundings like a cat will do from a window ledge, or a cougar from a
mountaintop. Only when it is ready to move on will it do so, traveling from
destination to destination while remaining a source of mystery, much like a cat,
wherever it goes.

Patterns

I would be the pink and silver as I ran along the paths,/And he would stumble after,

Bewildered by my laughter./I should see the sun flashing from his sword-hilt and
the buckles on his shoes./I would choose/To lead him in a maze along the patterned
paths.
Underneath the fallen blossom/In my bosom,
Is a letter I have hid./It was brought to me this morning by a rider from the Duke

- 66 -

"Madam, we regret to inform you that Lord Hartwell/Died in action Thursday se'nnight.
In a month he would have been my husband./In a month, here, underneath this lime,
We would have broke the pattern;/He for me, and I for him,
He as Colonel, I as Lady,/On this shady seat./He had a whim
That sunlight carried blessing./And I answered, "It shall be as you have said."
Now he is dead.

In Amy Lowell's "Patterns," she describes a passionate young woman confined by the rigidity of Victorian society, to behave in a proper manner at all time, which means never expressing emotion to others. On the outside, she does as society expects, but on the inside she feels confined and wishes to break free. The reader is introduced to the fact that the speaker has a fiancé whom she loves very much. She imagines leading him "in a maze along the patterned paths" of the garden, thereby breaking free from the Victorian boundaries. She longs for her future with this man in which she can live her life the way she wishes, and not in the "pattern" of society's expectations. Sadly, she has received word that her fiancé has died at war. She withholds showing emotion upon learning this devastating news, as expected, and now must continue in the prison cell of patterns, questioning why they must exist at all.

To the Stone-Cutters

Stone-cutters fighting time with marble, you fore-defeated
Challengers of oblivion
Eat cynical earnings, knowing rock splits, records fall down,
The square-limbed Roman letters
Scale in the thaws, wear in the rain. The poet as well
Builds his monument mockingly:
For man will be blotted out, the blithe earth dies, the brave sun
Die blind, his heart blackening:
Yet stones have stood for a thousand years, and pained thoughts found
The honey peace in old poems.

In Robinson Jeffers's poem "To the Stone-Cutters," Jeffers sets the tone immediately by acknowledging human mortality and the "foredefeated challengers of oblivion." Though the stone-cutters fight time with marble, the battle is futile, as "rock splits, records fall down / the square-limbed Roman letters / Scale in the thaws, wear in the rain." He continues the defeated tone by using the blithe earth and the brave sun to show that man's fate is predetermined, and the relentless effects of time are inescapable. But this does not transform into a pessimistic worldview. Though decidedly fatalistic, acceptance and a tinge of hope are apparent. Though men know their fate of dying is unavoidable, human beings are persistent in asserting their importance. Yes, their efforts will eventually be erased by the ebb and flow of time, but "stones have stood for a thousand years." Sometimes human efforts do impact many future generations. Although not measurable against the backdrop of eternity, these efforts play an important role for an allotted time.

Heat

O wind, rend open the heat,
cut apart the heat,
rend it to tatters.

Fruit cannot drop
through this thick air—
fruit cannot fall into heat
that presses up and blunts
the points of pears
and rounds the grapes.

Cut the heat—
plough through it,
turning it on either side
of your path.

"Heat," by H. D., relates a mundane request that many people commonly make relating to the seasons. In the midst of a heat wave, one wishes—or prays—for rain as well as for a breath of fresh air. In this poem, however, H. D. elevates the request into a poetic occasion, one that provides readers a focus for intense contemplation. The poem opens with an address or appeal to nature. "O wind, rend open the heat,/ cut apart the heat,/ rend it to tatters." The poetic voice makes the immediate request in pounding, aggressive and compact lines and follows with a number of direct assertions—fruit cannot even fall in heat this intense, the poem states. The compression of the poem seems to reinforce the close air and the poem's concluding plea to the wind: "Cut the heat—/ plough through it,/ turning it on either side/ of your path."

Velvet Shoes

Let us walk in the white snow
In a soundless space;
With footsteps quiet and slow,
At a tranquil pace,
Under veils of white lace.

I shall go shod in silk,
And you in wool,
White as white cow's milk,
More beautiful
Than the breast of a gull.

We shall walk through the still town
In a windless peace;
We shall step upon white down,
Upon silver fleece,
Upon softer than these.

We shall walk in velvet shoes:
Wherever we go
Silence will fall like dews
On white silence below.
We shall walk in the snow.

The most prominent metaphor in Elinor Wylie's "Velvet Shoes" is the adjective "white," representing the purity of the world. She selects several words preceded by "white" to stress their innocence and purity. "White snow" represents a pure world, one in which she invites the reader to walk with her with great care. Protection is provided in the form of "white lace," a metaphor for shelter to those who walk through the world in purity. The lines "I shall go shod in silk, And you in wool" employ the use of two natural fibers, silk and wool, considered to be pure and therefore ideal clothing for those walking in innocence. "White as the white cow's milk" again represents purity, with milk also representing nurturing. "Velvet shoes" provides vivid imagery to describe the care with which they will walk through the world, delicately and quietly to preserve its perfection. The message of the poem: If people take care of their beautiful, perfect world, it will protect, shelter and nurture them.

Bells for John Whiteside's Daughter

There was such speed in her little body,/And such lightness in her footfall,
It is no wonder her brown study/Astonishes us all.
Her wars were bruited in our high window./We looked among orchard trees and beyond
Where she took arms against her shadow,/Or harried unto the pond
The lazy geese, like a snow cloud/Dripping their snow on the green grass,
Tricking and stopping, sleepy and proud,/Who cried in goose, Alas,
For the tireless heart within the little/Lady with rod that made them rise
From their noon apple-dream and scuttle/Goose-fashion under the skies!
But now go the bells, and we are ready,/In one house we are stern stopped
To say we are vexed at her brown study,/Lying so primly propped.

In "Bells for John Whiteside's Daughter," by John Crowe Ransom, the occasion for the "bells" is the funeral of John Whiteside's young daughter. This poem, which serves as her elegy, describes the community's astonishment at the unexpected death of this little girl. However, rather than dwelling on the sadness of the present, and lamenting a future without her, the poem instead focuses on the past and the

- 69 -

active life she lived. Watching her at play from an upstairs window, the speaker—probably a neighbor, remembers her speed and lightness as she frolicked and played, taking "arms against her shadow," and making the geese rise and scuttle from "their noon apple-dream." The only time the speaker takes the reader to the present is with the mention of her brown study. The elegy offers not words of mourning, but reflections of happier times that indirectly confront one of the inexplicable mysteries of the world—a child's death.

Ode to the Confederate Dead

Row after row with strict impunity
The headstones yield their names to the element,
The wind whirrs without recollection;
In the riven troughs the splayed leaves
Pile up, of nature the casual sacrament
To the seasonal eternity of death;

Autumn is desolation in the plot
Of a thousand acres where these memories grow
From the inexhaustible bodies that are not
Dead, but feed the grass row after rich row.
Think of the autumns that have come and gone!—
Ambitious November with the humors of the year,
With a particular zeal for every slab,
Staining the uncomfortable angels that rot
On the slabs, a wing chipped here, an arm there:
The brute curiosity of an angel's stare
Turns you, like them, to stone,
Transforms the heaving air
Till plunged to a heavier world below
You shift your sea-space blindly
Heaving, turning like the blind crab.

In Allen Tate's "Ode to the Confederate Dead," the speaker happens upon a Confederate cemetery on a windy autumn day. Standing outside the cemetery, he notices "row after row" of headstones yielding the soldiers' names. On this blustery autumn day, he sees the dead leaves being lifted by the wind, reminding him of the cycle of life: "Think of the autumns that have come and gone!" He believes these buried Civil War heroes will be remembered, but notices how the leaves have stained "the uncomfortable angels" in the cemetery, that their wings are chipped, arms broken off, and he realizes that like the stone angels, the heroes will fade from existence like the names on their headstones. What is left—their physical bodies—will be erased from existence by nature. The speaker realizes that if these soldiers are forgotten in death, how much more easily he will be forgotten, having made no contribution in life as significant as theirs.

The Wasteland

April is the cruellest month, breeding
Lilacs out of the dead land, mixing
Memory and desire, stirring
Dull roots with spring rain.
Winter kept us warm, covering
Earth in forgetful snow, feeding
A little life with dried tubers.
Summer surprised us, coming over the Starnbergersee
With a shower of rain; we stopped in the colonnade,
And went on in sunlight, into the Hofgarten,
And drank coffee, and talked for an hour.
Bin gar keine Russin, stamm' aus Litauen, echt deutsch.
And when we were children, staying at the archduke's,
My cousin's, he took me out on a sled,
And I was frightened. He said, Marie,
Marie, hold on tight. And down we went.
In the mountains, there you feel free.
I read, much of the night, and go south in the winter.

In T. S. Eliot's "The Wasteland," lines 1–18 collectively discuss the natural cycle of death, symbolized by the passing of the seasons. April symbolizes a stage of limbo, when nature is neither living nor dead. The poem shifts from spring to summer, in which the speaker retells the
first meeting she had with her lover. "Bin gar keine Russin, stamm' aus Litauen, echt deutsch," means "I'm not Russian, I'm German," then she proceeds to tell her lover her childhood stories. In retelling these stories, the reader learns her name is "Marie" and that she is an aristocrat. Though the first stanza contains beautiful imagery, horrifying images are depicted throughout the rest of the poem to create a vision of the world we live in as a "wasteland." Because of the time the poem was written, Eliot also invokes images of the fairly recent World War I with German phrases, later depicting the casualties of the war.

Music I Heard

Music I heard with you was more than music,
And bread I broke with you was more than bread;
Now that I am without you, all is desolate;
All that was once so beautiful is dead.
Your hands once touched this table and this silver,
And I have seen your fingers hold this glass.
These things do not remember you, belovèd, —
And yet your touch upon them will not pass.
For it was in my heart you moved among them,
And blessed them with your hands and with your eyes;

And in my heart they will remember always, —
They knew you once, O beautiful and wise.

"Music I Heard," by Conrad Aiken, is a deeply romantic poem in which the speaker recalls how much "more" everything was when shared with his deceased loved one. Her presence made music and shared meals something more than simply what they were, something that cannot be experienced now that he is alone. As the speaker looks at the table where they listened to music and dined together, he can look at the objects on the table and recall his loved one's hands on them. And though the objects do not remember her, his heart will never forget. They too knew her once, and when he looks at these objects, he sees clearly the memory of her.

The Emperor of Ice-Cream

Call the roller of big cigars,
The muscular one, and bid him whip
In kitchen cups concupiscent curds.
Let the wenches dawdle in such dress
As they are used to wear, and let the boys
Bring flowers in last month's newspapers.
Let be be finale of seem.
The only emperor is the emperor of ice-cream.

Take from the dresser of deal,
Lacking the three glass knobs, that sheet
On which she embroidered fantails once
And spread it so as to cover her face.
If her horny feet protrude, they come
To show how cold she is, and dumb.
Let the lamp affix its beam.
The only emperor is the emperor of ice-cream.

Wallace Stevens's "The Emperor of Ice-Cream" depicts a funeral scene, while commenting on the human fallibilities of those attending the wake. The interpretations of this poem are many, as it was written in a way to allow the reader's personal opinion to dictate how they interpret the poem. The intent is to provoke an analysis and to allow the reader to closely look at the attitudes and actions of those who gather to pay their last respects. In "The Emperor of Ice-Cream," the festivities that are taking place at this particular wake express a sentiment that though a woman lies dead, life goes on. The "emperor of ice-cream" may be a contemptuous perception that ice-cream is more respectable than this crowd of so-called mourners, or a permissive one in which even the frivolities of life go on, even when the deceased is someone as important as a powerful emperor.

An Egyptian Pulled Glass Bottle in the Shape of a Fish

Here we have thirst/And patience, from the first,
And art, as in a wave held up for us to see/In its essential perpendicularity;

Not brittle but/Intense—the spectrum, that
Spectacular and nimble animal the fish,/Whose scales turn aside the sun's sword with their polish.

Marianne Moore's "An Egyptian Pulled Glass Bottle in the Shape of a Fish" is a poem that traces the process of creation, leading to the conclusion of the bottle. But it is also establishing criteria pertaining to art, which can also be applied to poetry. The poem begins with the alignment of thirst, patience and art within the object the speaker is contemplating. The first stanza concludes that art simply demands appreciation, while the second stanza appreciates what the artist has created. She observes that the work of art is genuine. This bottle not only aids in alleviating thirst, but it is a fish, created more perfectly even than its living model because it is glass, perfected by art. Just as its "scales turn aside the sun's sword with their polish," so the perfect poem is a reflecting, protecting and diverse surface.

The Red Wheelbarrow

"The Red Wheelbarrow," by William Carlos Williams, exemplifies the Imagist philosophy popular during his time, in which things, not ideas, are the subject of literary focus. This style forgoes traditional British stress patterns, and creates a typical "American" image. The pictorial style in which the poem is written owes much to the photographs of Alfred Stieglitz and Charles Sheeler, whom Williams met shortly before composing the poem. At this time the Imagist philosophy was only ten years old. The poem is an exercise in exemplifying the importance of the ordinary. Through "The Red Wheelbarrow," Williams states that a poem must not be realism, but reality itself, and by representing an object, this poem also represents an early stage in Williams's evolution as a poet.

Countee Cullen

Harlem Renaissance poet Countee Cullen had great esteem for the English Romantic poet John Keats. He shows this appreciation for Keats's poetry, and conviction that Keats's spirit lives on beyond physical death with his tributes, "To Endymion," "To John Keats, Poet" and "For John Keats, Apostle of Beauty." Throughout many of Cullen's works, the influence of Keats can be seen in his use of imagery, rhyme schemes and classical mythology. Both men revealed through their writings a sense of death's impending yet beautiful quality, and a heightened sense of life's mixture of joy and pain. However, while Keats focused primarily on an unhappy world, Cullen focused more on unhappy people. Keats revealed a viewpoint of an unjust world, whereas Cullen had a sense of cruelty that stems more specifically from the human heart. But both Cullen and Keats recognized that harsh truths at times must be faced, and at other times, avoided.

My People

The night is beautiful,
So the faces of *my people*.
The stars are beautiful,
So the eyes of *my people*
Beautiful, also, is the sun.
Beautiful, also, are the souls of *my people*.

"My People," by Langston Hughes, was written during a time in American literature known as the Harlem Renaissance. Hughes was one of the earliest innovators of the new literary art form, jazz poetry, having been raised on jazz music and black spirituals. The Harlem Renaissance sought to give African Americans, having been so recently enslaved, a strong voice with which they could express themselves in the new America. Hughes explored the black human condition, with a strong focus in the areas of struggle, joy, laughter and music, seeking to reeducate his audience as well as other artists. His poetry and fiction generally centered on the working-class lives of blacks in America, but his insights illuminated not only the Negro condition in America, but that of all humankind.

Fugitives

The Fugitives, formed shortly after World War I at Vanderbilt University in Nashville, Tennessee, were a group of young poets and critics. The group was led by poet and critic John Crowe Ransom, and included the poet, essayist and critic Donald Davidson, and the novelist and poet Robert Penn Warren. From the Fugitives came Crowe's bimonthly magazine, *The Fugitive*, which ran from 1922 through 1925 and was devoted to the writing and discussion of poetry. Contributors included Robert Graves and Hart Crane, among many others. The poetry magazine became a national phenomenon, and was often used in the university classroom.

The Waste Land

"The Waste Land," by T. S. Eliot, is considered by many critics to be the most important work of the modernist period, due to the influence it had in shaping some of the 20th century's most profound literary figures. Significantly influenced by Eliot's first wife Vivien and his friend Ezra Pound, "The Waste Land," with the help of Pound, was edited from its original 800-line draft to 434 lines. Setting the dark and haunting tone is the very first and famous line, "April is the cruelest month," similar to the method in which Chaucer set the tone for *The Canterbury Tales*. Many view the poem as a reflection of Eliot's disillusionment with civilization's moral decline in the post-World War I era; and although its point remains highly disputed still today, the inarguable constant is the disjointed style, with abrupt changes of speaker, disconnected thoughts and sudden changes in time and location.

Literary Devices

It May Not Always Be so

it may not always be so; and i say
that if your lips, which i have loved, should touch
another's, and your dear strong fingers clutch
his heart, as mine in time not far away;
if on another's face your sweet hair lay
in such silence as i know, or such
great writhing words as, uttering overmuch,
stand helplessly before the spirit at bay;

if this should be, i say if this should be—
you of my heart, send me a little word;
that i may go unto him, and take his hands,
saying, Accept all happiness from me.
Then shall i turn my face and hear one bird
sing terribly afar in the lost lands

"It May Not Always Be So," by E. E. Cummings, is a poem about letting go of someone you love, selflessly accepting the pain of losing someone in return for seeing them happy. E. E. Cummings's writing represented a new departure in poetry, the post-World War I era when love in literature became daring and celebrated. Focusing more on stylistic exploration, E. E. Cummings's poems challenged readers by intentionally subverting the very rules of grammar that the English language was built upon, presenting a new style of poetry that dealt less with conscious topics and more with associations and dreamlike images. Cummings's refusal to use capital letters in his poems is the most obvious characteristic found in his writings that demonstrates his rebellion and unconventionality. But also an artist, Cummings was deliberate in selecting the right typography and layout for his poems, conveying images and feelings by indirect allusions. Cummings's poetry has an avid following due to its ability to touch the hearts of people directly.

Thirteen Ways of Looking at a Blackbird

In Wallace Stevens's "Thirteen Ways of Looking at a Blackbird," Stevens shows a connection between thought processes and understanding through the first-person perspective of a poet viewing a blackbird. Each stanza offers a new way he has perceived this blackbird. First, he writes about his physical perception of the blackbird as an observer. Secondly, he discusses his mental processes during this time. These are as the thoughts and perceptions of the blackbird itself, as what it must be like to be that bird. By the end, he has concluded that by seeing this blackbird, a connection has been made and the blackbird has become a part of him. The poem is thematically structured to bring about a fuller understanding of our own thought processes, and to make us aware of shortcomings within our egocentric thoughts. The inner language of symbols and metaphors is chosen with care to bring about enlightenment, and stress the fact that static belief inhibits growth and mars perception.

Contemporary Period (1945–Present)

Delta Wedding

Eudora Welty's *Delta Wedding* begins with nine-year-old Laura, who recently lost her mother, and is traveling from Jackson, Mississippi to attend her cousin Dabney Fairchild's wedding. The story follows Laura as she desperately tries to feel a sense of belonging with the Fairchilds. After following Laura's thoughts, the reader then takes up Aunt Ellen's point of view, then Dabney's, then Aunt Primrose's, until eventually all the family members are reflecting on, and reflecting one another. *Delta Wedding* is more a novel of anticipations and reactions than events, focusing on the lives of women, their domestic routines and their reasons for these routines. This study in the way families work together and contradict one another rarely permeates the outside world, and when it does, Welty captures an uneasiness of an era that was timeless and yet vanishing.

The Swimmer

"The Swimmer," by John Cheever, takes place in the affluent suburbs of Westchester County, New York. It opens at a cocktail party on a midsummer Sunday. Attending this party is Neddy Merrill, who fancies himself younger than his actual age, and decides he will swim home via a succession of public and private swimming pools between the party he is attending and his home. While at first he is excited about his idea and well-received by the neighbors on whose property he trespasses, he is soon dismayed when he finds the pool of his friend's home, the Welchers, is dry and their house for sale. He recognizes his memory must be failing, and the situation continues to deteriorate, as it seems months, maybe longer, have passed between pools. When he arrives home, he finds his house locked and deserted, his family gone. It is then the reader discovers that years have passed since he set out on his mission to swim home.

Invisible Man

In Ralph Ellison's *Invisible Man*, the main theme is the invisibility of the underdog. The "invisible man" is the unnamed African-American narrator of the story, who, although highly intelligent, considers himself socially invisible. As events unfold that take the narrator from the role of a successful college student to a hunted man, his initial suspicion about his own invisibility is confirmed because everyone along the way sees him as a stereotype, not a real person. By the end of the story, the narrator has gone from bemoaning his state of invisibility to embracing it, realizing there are a number of advantages to remaining inconspicuous. In part, it gives him the opportunity to write his story, play a role in the preservation of history, and possibly launch much-needed political and societal change.

The Mourners

The main character in Bernard Malamud's "The Mourners" is Kessler, an elderly man who lives alone in a decrepit apartment on the East Side. Kessler has long been out of touch with his family, but is not bothered by their 30-year separation. When a vindictive janitor complains about the condition of Kessler's apartment to the tenement landlord, Gruber, the wheels of Kessler's eviction are set in motion. When Italian neighbors who previously distanced themselves from Kessler see him sitting outside in the cold with his belongings, they are infuriated and help him back into his apartment. Having a change of heart and feeling a sense of responsibility, Gruber decides to assist Kessler in finding lodging at a public home. At the same moment he mourns his decision, he finds Kessler sitting on his apartment floor in apparent mourning. The sad events have made Kessler realize the tragedy of cutting himself off from his family, a loss for which he now feels intense grief.

A Silver Dish

Saul Bellow's "A Silver Dish" begins with 60-year-old Woody Selbst reflecting on the memory of his father, Morris "Pop" Selbst. Woody is recalling an event that took place when he was 17 years old. Morris, who needed to pay back his mistress before her husband discovered money was missing, takes Woody to the home of Mrs. Skoglund, a rich patron who was paying Woody's seminary tuition. Morris asks her for $50, and Mrs. Skoglund leaves the room to pray about it. While out of the room, Morris attempts to steal a silver dish, "just in case" Mrs. Skoglund does not give him the money. Woody tries to wrestle the silver dish from him unsuccessfully, and Mrs. Skoglund, oblivious to their scuffle, returns to say she will give him the money. Morris tells his son he returned the silver dish, but the next week it turns up missing, so he admits he pawned it. As a result of his father's actions, Woody is forced to leave the seminary.

The Man Who Studied Yoga

In Norman Mailer's "The Man Who Studied Yoga," the central theme is dissatisfaction with one's life. The main character, Sam Slovoda, writes for comic magazines and suffers from the common feeling of being overworked and underappreciated. Though he dreams of writing a great novel, he has difficulty organizing his thoughts, and gives up, believing that what he wants to say is too complex to effectively write. He also yearns for affairs with other women but does not act on his desires. According to Sam Slovoda, "many people are dissatisfied with the present, and either dream of the past or anticipate the future." Ultimately, Sam's outlook on life and frustration with the life he lives lead to immense dissatisfaction with his family, friends and, most of all, himself.

Sonny's Blues

"Sonny's Blues," by James Baldwin, tells the story of two brothers who lead very different lives, and how they come to understand each other. Each brother has followed a different path of the African-American experience. The narrator has assimilated into white society as much as possible, while his brother, Sonny, a talented musician, has just been arrested on heroin charges. Though on different paths, both feel the pain of racism and limits placed on their opportunities. The narrator decides that his brother, like him, feels the same pain, and comes to terms with this while watching Sonny play the piano. As a drink on the piano resembles the "cup of trembling" from the book of Isaiah, symbolizing Sonny's suffering, the narrator understands that through music, Sonny can turn his suffering into something worthwhile, and he grasps this commonality between them.

The Life You Save May be Your Own

Set on a desolate Southern plantation in 1944, Flannery O'Connor's "The Life You Save May Be Your Own" begins as carpenter Tom T. Shiftlet enters the lives of an old woman and her innocent daughter, Lucynell. Missing half of his left arm, Mr. Shiftlet is said to resemble a "crooked cross" as he stands outstretched, symbolizing his questionable moral character. After doing some work on the plantation, the old woman convinces Mr. Shiftlet to marry Lucynell. He does, but only because he wants their car. After the civil ceremony, Lucynell picks the cherries off her hat and throws them out the window, symbolizing her loss of innocence. Mr. Shiftlet drives to a diner, where he abandons Lucynell. As he drives away, the sky around him changes, and he sees a sign that reads, "Drive carefully. The life you save may be your own." The sign is his last warning that redemption is still possible, but he chooses to keep driving, rejecting salvation and continuing on the road to damnation.

The Glass Menagerie

Characters in Tennessee Williams's *The Glass Menagerie*:
- Amanda Wingfield
- Tom Wingfield
- Laura Wingfield
- Jim O'Connor
- Mr. Wingfield

The characters in Tennessee Williams's *The Glass Menagerie* consist of Amanda, Tom and Laura Wingfield, and Jim O'Connor. Amanda Wingfield is the mother of Tom and Laura, who pushes to find a husband for her daughter, while reflecting often on her past on the southern plantation farm. Laura Wingfield is Amanda's overly shy daughter and Tom's sister, who lives in her own private world. Tom Wingfield is Amanda's son and Laura's brother, who supports his family working at the shoe factory. Jim O'Connor is Tom's friend and co-worker, and he is invited to dinner as a potential "gentleman caller" for Laura. Though only his photograph is seen in the play, Mr. Wingfield is Amanda's husband, who deserted the family 16 years prior.

Death of a Salesman

Willy Loman is the main character in Arthur Miller's *Death of a Salesman*. An elderly salesman who works solely on commission, Willy does not make enough money to pay his bills, yet seems oblivious to this, as he lives in a world of false hopes and illusions. Willy has difficulty in his older age distinguishing the past from the present. He has flashbacks that center mostly around his son's Biff's senior year of high school, when Biff discovers Willy was having an affair during his sales trips, and loses respect for his father. Willy believes that being well liked equates success, and this illusion ultimately results in his demise. In the end, Willy commits suicide, believing he is worth more dead than alive, so Biff can have his insurance money and achieve success. Willy is never able to see a realistic picture of himself and his sons, but he is also portrayed as a victim of a free enterprise society in which he was spent like "a piece of fruit."

Big Black Good Man

In Richard Wright's "Big Black Good Man," contrasts in race between Olaf and Jim are extreme. Olaf is described as the whitest of white, while Jim is described as "blue-black" in color. Portrayed as racist, Olaf harbors deep-seated jealousy and resentment toward Jim, as Jim is younger, stronger and wealthy. He does not acknowledge Jim as a person, and never uses his name. Jim, however, has no interest in Olaf due to Olaf's age and low social position, but treats him with decency as a human being. Though Olaf harbors hatefulness, and Jim does not, Olaf leads a moral life as a hard-working married man. And though Jim is free of prejudice, he drinks heavily and spends every night with a prostitute. Jim recognizes Olaf as a good man because he helped him by sending him Lena, and Olaf finally comes to see Jim more accurately, calling him a "big black good man." The story leaves the reader to ponder the truly accurate measures of a man's goodness.

To Kill a Mockingbird

Harper Lee's *To Kill a Mockingbird* is a story about prejudice, and two children who learn that no matter how unfair or subtle the prejudice might be, it is a reality of the world. Set in 1930s Alabama, Scout Finch and her brother, Jem, who initially are out to taunt the neighborhood recluse, Boo Radley, befriend him and come to understand that he deserves to live in peace. Meanwhile, Scout and Jem's father, Atticus, is subjected to the town's scorn for defending a black man, Tom Robinson, accused of a crime he did not commit. One night, Bob Ewell, the white man who accuses Tom of raping his daughter, attacks Scout and Jem on their way home from a Halloween party, and they are rescued by Boo Radley. To protect Boo, the sheriff decides that Bob fell on his own knife while attacking Jem. Over two years, Scout learns the evil of prejudice, and that no one is less or better than anyone else.

True West

True West, by Sam Shepard, is the tale of two brothers who lead very different lives. Austin is a successful screenwriter and family man. His brother Lee is an alcoholic and thief. While Austin is house-sitting for his vacationing mother so he can work on his screenplay and meet with Hollywood producer Saul Kimmer, Lee drops in unexpectedly and announces he too will be staying there, as he plans to rob his mother's neighbors. When Saul arrives the next day to talk with Austin, Lee convinces him to play golf, and pitches a movie idea to the producer, which he agrees to make. Lee then takes over the role of frustrated screenwriter, while Austin begins drinking and goes on a stealing spree. On one level, *True West* is a story about sibling strife, and on another, it is about the search for identity amidst a highly dysfunctional family.

Separating

John Updike's "Separating" is a short story revolving around the breakup of Richard and Joan Maple's marriage, or more specifically, the careful strategy and planning that has gone into how they will convey the news to their four teenage children. As they are faced with this dilemma, Richard believes they should tell them as a group, and Joan believes they should tell them individually, as they will each have their own individual reaction. But for all of their planning, the truth comes out in a dinner celebration. For months, Richard and Joan have concealed the reality of their situation from their children, pretending as though nothing is wrong. And when the truth finally is revealed, they minimize the situation, making it appear as though this is just a trial separation. Throughout the story, Updike uses the clay tennis court to symbolize the happy times of the past and the current disintegration of the marriage, painting a picture of flaws, fractures and paralyzed emotions.

Poems and Prose

Dream Song 1

Huffy Henry hid the day/unappeasable Henry sulked.
I see his point,—a trying to put things over.
It was the thought that they thought/they could *do* it made Henry wicked & away.
But he should have come out and talked.

All the world like a woolen lover/once did seem on Henry's side.
Then came a departure.
Thereafter nothing fell out as it might or ought.
I don't see how Henry, pried/open for all the world to see, survived.

What he has now to say is a long/wonder the world can bear & be.
Once in a sycamore I was glad/all at the top, and I sang.
Hard on the land wears the strong sea/and empty grows every bed.

John Berryman's "Dream Song 1" begins with a speaker who knows Henry inside and out, physically describing him as "huffy" and recognizing when he is sulking. Though this speaker sees Henry's point for not coming out and talking, they also recognize that by not doing so, he made the wrong choice, and therefore, sealed his fate. The transition into the second stanza makes it clear why Henry is of sullen mood. The world was once on his side, but something has changed—perhaps something devastating, creating a wound that pried Henry "open for all the world to see." In the final stanza there is a lament for past happiness from atop a sycamore tree. And although once the world was like a "woolen lover" in stanza two, stanza three reflects sadly on a now empty bed.

Traveling Through the Dark

Traveling through the dark I found a deer/dead on the edge of the Wilson River road.
It is usually best to roll them into the canyon:/that road is narrow; to swerve might make more dead.

By glow of the tail-light I stumbled back of the car/and stood by the heap, a doe, a recent killing;
she had stiffened already, almost cold./I dragged her off; she was large in the belly.

My fingers touching her side brought me the reason—/her side was warm; her fawn lay there waiting,
alive, still, never to be born./Beside that mountain road I hesitated.

The car aimed ahead its lowered parking lights;/under the hood purred the steady engine
I stood in the glare of the warm exhaust turning red;/around our group I could hear the wilderness listen.

I thought hard for us all—my only swerving—,/then pushed her over the edge into the river.

"Traveling in the Dark," by William Stafford, begins with the speaker introducing an event that has just occurred. Driving his car on a dark, winding road, the driver sees a deer that has been struck by a car, and decides the best course of action is to roll it into the canyon, making the road safe for other drivers. In stanza two, the speaker goes to the back of the car to examine the deer. Though she is already almost cold, he notices the doe is pregnant. In stanza three, he realizes the fawn inside her is still alive, as "her side was warm." This revelation causes him to hesitate and reconsider, as there is another life at stake, almost ready to be born. As he pauses in contemplation in stanza four, the wilderness listens. In stanza five, realizing the choices are as narrow as the road he is on, he decides he must push her over the edge for the same reason he initially came to that conclusion.

Fork

This strange thing must have crept
Right out of hell.
It resembles a bird's foot
Worn around the cannibal's neck.

As you hold it in your hand,
As you stab with it into a piece of meat,
It is possible to imagine the rest of the bird:
Its head which like your fist
Is large, bald, beakless, and blind.

In Charles Simic's poem "Fork," the author uses a simple object, a fork, to make a statement about underlying violence in contemporary society. A surrealist, Simic transforms an instrument normally associated with civility and etiquette, stripping it of social significance and transforming it into an instrument of barbarism. By doing so, this simple utensil is no longer an image of politeness, but an extension of humanity's violent nature. At odds with the formality of dining, the fork is a murderer, stabbing "into a piece of meat," symbolizing victimization as humans inflict pain and violence on other humans. By distorting the ordinary, Simic tears away a civilized veneer and reshapes how the reader visualizes the fork, thus criticizing the cycle of violence that continues to plague humanity, even in civilized society.

Morning Song

Love set you going like a fat gold watch./The midwife slapped your footsoles, and your bald cry
Took its place among the elements.
Our voices echo, magnifying your arrival. New statue./In a drafty museum, your nakedness
Shadows our safety. We stand round blankly as walls.
I'm no more your mother/Than the cloud that distills a mirror to reflect its own slow
Effacement at the wind's hand.
All night your moth-breath/Flickers among the flat pink roses. I wake to listen:
A far sea moves in my ear.
One cry, and I stumble from bed, cow-heavy and floral/In my Victorian nightgown.

Your mouth opens clean as a cat's. The window square
Whitens and swallows its dull stars. And now you try/Your handful of notes;
The clear vowels rise like balloons.

"Morning Song," by Sylvia Plath, portrays both the bond and the individuality of a mother and her newborn child. In the first stanza, she compares her baby's conception to the setting of a watch, the timer of life beginning, but also something that was created by "love." In the second stanza, the mother compares the baby to a "new statue" in a "drafty museum," indicating a distance she feels, the way an observer in a museum may feel toward the subjects. The feeling that the baby is somehow foreign to her is indicated as well in the third stanza, as she proclaims she is "no more your mother" than a cloud is responsible for its mirror image formed from the water it produces. She recognizes the baby's individuality. Stanza four, however, depicts the closeness she feels in responding to her baby's cries, and in the final stanza, she compares the cries, the "morning song," to rising balloons that will ascend out of her reach.

Aunt Jennifer's Tigers

Aunt Jennifer's tigers prance across a screen,/Bright topaz denizens of a world of green.
They do not fear the men beneath the tree;/They pace in sleek chivalric certainty.
Aunt Jennifer's finger fluttering through her wool/Find even the ivory needle hard to pull.
The massive weight of Uncle's wedding band/Sits heavily upon Aunt Jennifer's hand.

When Aunt is dead, her terrified hands will lie/Still ringed with ordeals she was mastered by.

The tigers in the panel that she made/Will go on prancing, proud and unafraid.

"Aunt Jennifer's Tigers," by Adrienne Rich, depicts Aunt Jennifer, a woman filled with passion and creative fire, but struggling to accept the weight of her role in life. Though she feels unable to rise above a life defined by rules, she does find a way to attain some sense of immortality, through sewing, and more specifically, the tigers she is sewing. Aunt Jennifer's tigers represent freedom and power, things she longs for in her own life, as they tread through their world. They "prance" as opposed to merely treading through the jungle. The second stanza then provides a bleak picture of how Aunt Jennifer feels burdened by her role, her spirit suffering the weight of the world. Her death is described as an event that, too, holds no hope. But the tigers she has made will remain perpetually "prancing, proud and unafraid." Even in art, Aunt Jennifer is not free to express herself like the tigers of the jungle.

Why I Am Not a Painter

Well,/for instance, Mike Goldberg /is starting a painting. I drop in.
"Sit down and have a drink" he/says. I drink; we drink. I look
up. "You have SARDINES in it." /"Yes, it needed something there."
"Oh." I go and the days go by /and I drop in again. The painting is
finished. "Where's SARDINES?"/All that's left is just /letters, "It was too much," Mike
says.

But me? One day I am thinking of /a color: orange. I write a line
about orange. Pretty soon it is a /whole page of words, not lines.
Then another page. There should be/so much more, not of orange, of
words, of how terrible orange is /and life. Days go by. My poem
is finished and I haven't mentioned /orange yet. It's twelve poems, I call
it ORANGES. And one day in a gallery /I see Mike's painting, called SARDINES.

"Why I Am Not a Painter," by Frank O'Hara, reflects upon and compares the creative
process of painting versus writing. Told in first person from O'Hara's point of view,
O'Hara depicts in narrative form his friend Mike Goldberg's painting in various
stages. He first notices the word "SARDINES" in the painting, but realizes the word
has been removed upon the painting's completion. Likewise, O'Hara composes
twelve pastorals from the starting point of the color orange, yet fails to use
"oranges" in any of his writings. Though inspired by something specific, the poem
reveals that the original inspiration, though not contained in the finished works, was
granted the honor of title, with Goldberg's painting entitled "SARDINES" and
O'Hara's poems entitled, "ORANGES." The poem also reflects on how art and
everyday life go together through O'Hara's visits with Goldberg.

Some Trees

These are amazing: each /Joining a neighbor, as though speech
Were a still performance. /Arranging by chance
To meet as far this morning/From the world as agreeing
With it, you and I /Are suddenly what the trees try
To tell us we are: /That their merely being there
Means something; that soon /We may touch, love, explain.
And glad not to have invented /Some comeliness, we are surrounded:
A silence already filled with noises, /A canvas on which emerges
A chorus of smiles, a winter morning. /Place in a puzzling light, and moving,
Our days put on such reticence /These accents seem their own defense.

"Some Trees," by John Ashbery, is a poem that examines how thought and feeling
interact with the world to create art. The title, "Some Trees," indicates there is no
guarantee that any other trees will offer epiphanies, just "some trees," like these
particular pillars of nature. He begins the poem with the statement, "These are
amazing," perhaps not for any particular reason other than they are looked upon as

such, in part because they are "each/Joining a neighbor." And though joined, they are apart, rooted in place, without the ability to move closer to each other. The mute trees speak, a "still performance" in nature's temple, and try to tell us that they mean something. This meaning could be the possibility of joy, the hope as they proclaim, "soon/We may touch, love, explain." The words issued are confused, as speech in this case is merely a still performance, and the still performance is speech as the reader contemplates what, if anything, it means.

Separation

Your absence has gone through me
Like thread through a needle.
Everything I do is stitched with its color.

"Separation," by W. S. Merwin, is a poem that, in very few words, captures the emotion of separation. Beginning with what the reader is led to believe will be a familiar cliché, such as "gone through me like a knife," the wording takes an unexpected turn by using "thread through a needle" to depict this emotion. Rather than using a sharp object that would place the emphasis of the poem on the emotion of pain, it instead focuses on the feeling of separation itself. Taking another unexpected turn, rather than using an analogy that clearly depicts something being separated, Merwin describes being apart as a kind of sewing together. So just as traces of thread are left everywhere by the needle, everything the speaker does is marked by the absence of the person who is gone.

Lying in a Hammock

Over my head, I see the bronze butterfly/Asleep on the black trunk,
Blowing like a leaf in green shadow./Down the ravine behind the empty house,
The cowbells follow one another/Into the distances of the afternoon.
To my right,/In a field of sunlight between two pines,
The droppings of last year's horses Blaze up into golden stones.
I lean back, as the evening darkens and comes on.
A chicken hawk floats over, looking for home.
I have wasted my life.

As the title indicates in James Wright's "Lying in a Hammock," the speaker spends a lazy late afternoon lying in a hammock, noticing his surroundings. He views a "bronze butterfly," hears the cowbells, sees horse droppings illuminated by sunlight "between two pines," and spots a chicken hawk flying overhead in search of home. The vivid imagery of life, sounds, decay and looking for home are abruptly ended with his surprising declaration, "I have wasted my life." "Lying in a Hammock" depicts a sad realization in the midst of an otherwise happy moment. Perhaps the speaker has wasted his life on things that did not matter, never stopping to pay attention to his surroundings. Bittersweet, the poem relays the importance of relishing those short intervals of happiness found in simplicity, before, like the chicken hawk, we head back home.

Her Kind

I have gone out, a possessed witch,/haunting the black air, braver at night;
dreaming evil, I have done my hitch/over the plain houses, light by light:
lonely thing, twelve-fingered, out of mind./A woman like that is not a woman, quite.
I have been her kind.
I have found the warm caves in the woods,/filled them with skillets, carvings, shelves,
closets, silks, innumerable goods;/fixed the suppers for the worms and the elves:
whining, rearranging the disaligned./A woman like that is misunderstood.
I have been her kind.

I have ridden in your cart, driver,/waved my nude arms at villages going by,
learning the last bright routes, survivor/where your flames still bite my thigh
and my ribs crack where your wheels wind./A woman like that is not ashamed to die.
I have been her kind.

In Anne Sexton's "Her Kind," the speaker is an outcast woman who embraces society's negative stereotype of modern women, transforming it into a positive image. In the first stanza, she establishes herself as a witch, not literally, but as the persona used to exemplify the role of liberated women in society. The voice of society expresses the opinion that modern women, like witches, are evil, while the speaker sarcastically mimics public opinion. In the second stanza, she lives as an outsider in "warm caves in the woods" and states, "a woman like that is misunderstood" by a society that cannot see her point of view. The third stanza alludes to the torture of witches, with the phrase "still bite" stressing that torture still remains, but has merely changed shape. "A woman like that is not ashamed to die" because everyone already believes she is crazy, or evil, and her reputation is already harmed.

My Papa's Waltz

The whiskey on your breath /Could make a small boy dizzy;
But I hung on like death:/Such waltzing was not easy.

We romped until the pans/ Slid from the kitchen shelf;
My mother's countenance/ Could not unfrown itself.

The hand that held my wrist/ Was battered on one knuckle;
At every step you missed/ My right ear scraped a buckle.

You beat time on my head/ With a palm caked hard by dirt,
Then waltzed me off to bed/ Still clinging to your shirt.

Theodore Roethke's poem "My Papa's Waltz" inspires much debate as to its meaning. One interpretation popular in modern times is that it depicts child abuse. A father drunkenly beats his son, making him dizzy, knocking pans off the kitchen shelf, battered on one knuckle from the struggle, and hitting him with a belt, while the mother frowns in disapproval but is otherwise ambivalent. Read simply, however, the subject of the poem simply is a father who has been drinking, and engages in a playful waltz with his son. He stumbles, knocking over mother's pans— upon which she frowns—as the boy hangs on "like death," but endures the dance that takes place between him and this much loved parent. The boy is about waist high, thus the belt buckle scrapes his ear with every misstep, and as it's bedtime, the father continues the waltz while escorting his son to bed.

Historical and Social Settings

Ann Beattie

The works of author Ann Beattie speak for her generation, the children and teens of the 1960s who witnessed its altruism and turmoil, and who came to adulthood in the egocentric decade of the 1970s. Her first novel, *Chilly Scenes of Winter*, depicts characters who Beattie has explained feel let down, either due to their lack of involvement in the events surrounding the 1960s, or their heavy involvement, which they feel was to no avail. Most of the characters in Beattie's works are middle class, educated, live in the Middle Atlantic region or New England, and are surrounded by remnants of the past such as ex-lovers or spouses, inherited homes, and once popular music that is a constant part of the background. Though they yearn for romance that seems to evade them, have tedious jobs and irritating relatives, inaction is their response to the disillusionment they now feel.

Tennessee Williams

Though many of Tennessee Williams's most famous plays are set in the post-Civil War South, the embedded tensions, problems and conflicts between his characters deeply resonate with all human experience. A few of the characters created by Williams that transcend the Southern environment in which they are depicted are the "displaced" Blanche in *A Streetcar Named Desire*, Maggie in *Cat on a Hot Tin Roof*, as well as brother and sister Tom and Laura in *The Glass Menagerie*. Other writers who built themes around the old South's lost aristocracy and the tension created by invading materialism—an era of writing sometimes called "Southern Renaissance"—include William Faulkner, Flannery O'Connor and Robert Penn Warren. Through family quarrels, Tennessee Williams crafted powerful portraits of individuals dealing with spiritual displacement, loneliness and self-deception, themes also depicted by American dramatists Eugene O'Neill and Arthur Miller.

Allen Ginsberg

The poetry of Allen Ginsberg was strongly influenced by Modernism, specifically Ezra Pound, Hart Crane, T. S. Eliot and William Carlos Williams, as well as Romanticism, including the works of Percy Shelley and John Keats. Ginsberg studied poetry under William Carlos Williams, who taught him not to emulate old masters of poetry in rhyme and meter, but to speak with his own voice and that of the common American. Williams passed on his philosophy of "no ideas but in things" to Ginsberg, and his teachings created a tremendous shift in Ginsberg's poetry from a formalist to a loose, colloquial free-verse style. Ginsberg was influenced by Surrealists such as Antonin Artaud and Jean Genet, but he also claimed traditional influences such as Herman Melville, Edgar Allan Poe and Emily Dickinson. Ginsberg studied haiku, and the effect of contrasting two apparent opposites. He used this technique with two starkly different images, something weak with something strong, or something holy with something unholy.

Literary Devices

Toni Morrison

Similar to jazz in both dialogue and narration, the works of Toni Morrison have often been compared to jazz, but the similarity extends beyond just these elements. Morrison herself once noted that her approach to writing is similar to the way a jazz musician approaches music composition. Though the words play easily on the page, her work results from careful research and detailed historical settings, in much the same way the easy sound of jazz, notoriously complex and difficult to play, results from hours of practice and revision. Another literary device she employs that is similar to jazz is verbal "riffing," or "varying repetition," as well as improvisations in dialogue. Varying repetition or "echoing" of notes as well as improvisation are also common musical elements of jazz.

The Sandbox

Edward Albee's *The Sandbox* is a one-act play that serves as an extension of an allegory. It consists not of actual characters but caricatures, aware that they are merely symbols. They are aware of their presence onstage and understand the stereotypical emotions and rules they are meant to display to the audience. Albee has essentially illustrated Shakespeare's assessment that "all the world's a stage, and all men and women merely players" with caricatures who show that the traditional conception and reaction to death are contrived. The characters include Mommy, Daddy, Grandma, the Young Man and the Musician. The conversations of Mommy and Daddy set the tone of the play, conveying an air of preparation for Grandma's impending death; Grandma is in the sandbox, which represents her deathbed; the Young Man represents the Angel of Death; and the Musician is directed to start or stop playing music appropriate to the contrived emotion. *The Sand Box* demonstrates Albee's take on how society engages in role-playing in response to death.

Practice Test

Practice Questions

1. Which of the following is NOT a poem by Anne Bradstreet?
   a. "Before the Birth of One of Her Children"
   b. "Contemplations"
   c. "Upon the Burning of our House, July 10, 1666"
   d. "A Funeral Poem on the Death of C.E"
   e. "A Dialogue Between Old England and New"

2. The biblical phrase "city upon a hill" is also found in which of the following works?
   a. Jonathan Edwards' "Sinners in the Hands of an Angry God"
   b. William Bradford's "History of Plymouth Plantation"
   c. John Winthrop's "A Model of Christian Charity"
   d. Samuel Sewall's "The Diary of Samuel Sewall"
   e. Cotton Mather's "Magnalia Christi Americana"

3. Which of the following authors was dubbed "The Poet of the American Revolution"?
   a. Henry Wadsworth Longfellow
   b. Anne Bradstreet
   c. William Cullen Bryant
   d. Philip Freneau
   e. Ebenezer Cooke

4. Which of the following is NOT an example of a prominent form of Colonial American literature?
   a. Pamphlets extolling the benefits of the colonies
   b. Journals discussing religious foundations and disputes
   c. Writings describing interactions and conflicts with the Indians
   d. Patriotic poems and songs
   e. Novels depicting regional dialect

Question 5 pertains to the following excerpt:
> "About three o'clock afternoon, I begun my Journey from Boston to New-Haven; being about two Hundred Mile. My kinsman, Capt. Robert Luist, waited on me as farr as Dedham, where I was to meet y Western post."

5. The above passage is the first excerpt from which of the following works?
   a. "The Journal of Madam Knight" by Sarah Kemble Knight
   b. "The Narrative of the Captivity" by Mary Rowlandson
   c. "Upon the Burning of our House" by Anne Bradstreet
   d. "The Gleaner" by Judith Sargent Murray
   e. "A Farewell to America to Mrs. S.W." by Phillis Wheatley

6. Which of the following best describes James Fenimore Cooper's fictitious character Natty Bumppo?
   a. An outlaw who took part in the kidnapping of two pioneer sisters
   b. A desperate, southern character longing to escape from his circumstances
   c. A near-fearless warrior who grew up with Native Americans
   d. A New England minister who took a stand against slavery
   e. A captain in pursuit of an impossible catch

7. "A Pretty Story" by Francis Hopkinson can best be described as which of the following?
   a. The making of the American flag
   b. A skeptical examination of the relationship between Great Britain and the colonies
   c. A compilation of songs composed by Hopkinson
   d. Reflections on Hopkinson's life in Philadelphia
   e. An allegorical work likening the royal government to a tree

Question 8 pertains to the following excerpt:
> "Is life so dear, or peace so sweet, as to be purchased at the price of chains and slavery? Forbid it, Almighty God! I know not what course others may take; but as for me, give me liberty or give me death!"

8. The above passage ends the famous speech delivered by which of the following?
   a. Thomas Jefferson
   b. Patrick Henry
   c. Washington Irving
   d. Joseph Galloway
   e. John Winthrop

Question 9 pertains to the following passage:
> "I prize thy love more than whole Mines of gold
> Or all the riches that the East doth hold.
> My love is such that Rivers cannot quench,
> Nor ought but love from thee give recompense."

9. The above passage from Anne Bradstreet's "To My Dear and Loving Husband" represents which of the following two literary devices?
    a. Paradox and Simile
    b. Imagery and Irony
    c. Iambic Pentameter and Foreshadowing
    d. Hyperbole and Metaphor
    e. Personification and Parallelism

Question 10 pertains to the following passage:
    "Still was the night, Serene and Bright,
    when all Men sleeping lay;
    Calm was the season, and carnal reason
    thought so 'twould last for ay.
    Soul, take thine ease, let sorrow cease,
    much good thou hast in store:
    This was their Song, their Cups among,
    the Evening before."

10. The above passage from Michael Wigglesworth's "The Day of Doom" best describes which of the following?
    a. The security of the world before Christ's coming to judgment
    b. A description of man just before he awakens
    c. Christ's sheep separated from the goats
    d. A full moon on a summer evening
    e. The majesty of Christ's appearance on judgment day

11. Which of the following works provides a Loyalist interpretation of the Revolution?
    a. Increase Mather's "Case of Conscience"
    b. Thomas Jefferson's "A Summary View of the Rights of British America"
    c. Patrick Henry's "Give Me Liberty or Give Me Death"
    d. John Woolman's "Serious Considerations on Various Subjects of Importance"
    e. Joseph Galloway's "Historical and Political Reflections on the Rise and Progress of the American Rebellion"

Questions 12-13 refer to the same work
    "The bear that breathes the northern blast/ Did numb, torpedo-like, a wasp
    Whose stiffened limbs encramped, lay bathing/ In Sol's warm breath and shine as saving, / Which with her hands she chafes and stands / Rubbing her legs, shanks, thighs, and hands."

12. How can Edward Taylor's "Upon a Wasp Chilled with Cold" best be described based on the above excerpt?
    a. A seasonally descriptive poem
    b. A poem of detailed natural observation
    c. A romantic poem about love
    d. An epitaph to a departed loved one
    e. A pastoral depiction of nature

Question 13 pertains to the following excerpt:
> "Her warm thanks offering for all. / Lord, clear my misted sight that I
> May hence view Thy divinity, / Some sparks whereof thou up dost
> hasp/ Within this little downy wasp
> In whose small corporation we/ A school and a schoolmaster see".

13. How can the poem best be described based on this excerpt?
    a. A devotional poem
    b. A biographical poem
    c. A ballad
    d. A poem about authority
    e. A poem intended to make a politcal statement

14. Which of the following poems is one of the earliest examples of debunking and disillusionment, reflecting the author's own impressions of the barbarous colonial frontier?
    a. Philip Freneau's "On Mr. Paine's Rights of Man"
    b. Henry Wadsworth Longfellow's "Blind Bartimeus"
    c. Ebenezer Cooke's "The Sot-Weed Factor"
    d. William Cullen Bryant's "Thanatopsis"
    e. John Trumbull's "Beneath a Mountain's Brow"

Question 15 pertains to the following excerpt:
> "That fearful sound of 'Fire' and 'Fire!' / Let no man know is my
> desire"

15. The above excerpt from Anne Bradstreet's "Upon the Burning of Our House" can best be described as what?
    a. A plea for godly strength in the face of earthly distress
    b. Keeping a secret in the midst of tragedy
    c. Facing one's fear alone
    d. The speaker's goal to be prepared for the day of judgment
    e. A confession regarding tensions in the speaker's home

Question 16 pertains to the following passage:

"The following Tale was found among the papers of the late Diedrich Knickerbocker, an old gentleman of New York, who was very curious in the Dutch history of the province, and the manners of the descendants from its primitive settlers."

16. The above passage begins the story of which of the following?
   a. James Fenimore Cooper's "The Pioneers"
   b. Washington Irving's "The Legend of Sleepy Hollow"
   c. Thomas Paine's "The American Crisis"
   d. Sarah Kemble Knight's "The Journal of Madam Knight"
   e. Washington Irving's "Rip Van Winkle"

17. Nathaniel Hawthorne's "The Scarlett Letter" depicts a belief in individual choice and consequence. This ideal is a characteristic of which of the following?
   a. Realism
   b. Transcendentalism
   c. Romanticism
   d. Puritanism
   e. Naturalism

18. Which of the following is NOT a character in Mark Twain's "Adventures of Huckleberry Finn"?
   a. Widow Douglas
   b. Pap
   c. Tom Canty
   d. The Grangerfords
   e. Judge Thatcher

Question 19 pertains to the following passage:

"We paused before a house that seemed
A swelling of the ground;
The roof was scarcely visible,
The cornice but a mound."

19. In the above passage from Emily Dickinson's "Because I Could Not Stop for Death," the word "house" in the first line depicts which of the following?
   a. The house the speaker grew up in
   b. A church
   c. A school that burned down
   d. The speaker's tomb
   e. Heaven

20. "The Philosophy of Composition" was Edgar Allan Poe's follow-up essay detailing the creation of which of his works?
  a. "Annabel Lee"
  b. "The Raven"
  c. "The Fall of the House of Usher"
  d. "To Helen"
  e. "The Masque of the Red Death"

21. Romanticism in literature can best be defined as which of the following?
  a. A movement that seeks to replicate a believable everyday reality
  b. Literature that is either utilitarian, very personal, or religious
  c. The exaltation of senses and emotions over reason and intellect
  d. The presentation of details that are actually part of life
  e. The belief that intuition and conscience transcend experience

Questions 22-23 pertain to the following passage:
  "A noiseless patient spider,
  I mark'd where on a little promontory it stood, isolated,
  Mark'd how to explore the vacant vast surrounding,
  It launch'd forth filament, filament, filament, out of itself,
  Ever unreeling them, ever tirelessly speeding them."
  "And you O my Soul where you stand,
  Surrounded, detached, in measureless oceans of space,
  Ceaselessly musing, venturing, throwing, seeking the spheres to connect them,
  Till the bridge you will need be form'd, till the ductile anchor hold,
  Till the gossamer thread you fling catch somewhere, O my Soul."

22. Which of the following literary devices is used in the first stanza of Walt Whitman's "A Noiseless Patient Spider"?
  a. Alliteration
  b. Hyperbole
  c. Onomatopoeia
  d. Simile
  e. Paradox

23. Which is used in the second stanza of Whitman's poem?
  a. Parallelism
  b. Oxymoron
  c. Simile
  d. Metaphor
  e. Symbolism

24. Which of the following is NOT a theme of Herman Melville's "Moby Dick"?
    a. Man against nature
    b. Betrayal of a friend
    c. Revenge
    d. A mysterious power or force
    e. Pending doom

Question 25 pertains to the following passage:
    "To believe your own thought, to believe that what is true for you in your private heart is true for all men—that is genius."

25. The above statement is from which of the following works?
    a. Frederick Douglass' "My Bondage and My Freedom"
    b. Oliver Wendell Holmes' "Reflections of a Proud Pedestrian"
    c. Henry David Thoreau's "Civil Disobedience"
    d. James Russell Lowell's "Conversations on the Old Poets"
    e. Ralph Waldo Emerson's "Self-Reliance"

26. Which short story focuses on a conflict between two groups of American colonists?
    a. "The Big Bear of Arkansas" by T.B. Thorpe
    b. "A Week on the Concord and Merrimack Rivers" by Henry David Thoreau
    c. "The Child's Champion" by Walt Whitman
    d. "The Maypole of Merry Mount" by Nathaniel Hawthorne
    e. "The Supernaturalism of New England" by John Greenleaf Whittier

27. Henry David Thoreau's "Walden" CANNOT be described as which the following?
    a. His account of solitary living
    b. An exercise in understanding human characteristics
    c. Freedom of living in the natural world around him
    d. A manual for self-reliance
    e. His refusal to live by the rules of hard work in order to build wealth

Question 28 pertains to the following passage:
    "I died for Beauty – but was scarce
    Adjusted in the Tomb,
    When One who died for Truth, was lain
    In an adjoining room –
    He questioned softly "why I failed"?
    "For Beauty," I replied –
    "And I – for Truth – Themself are One –
    We Brethren, are," He said –
    And so, as Kinsmen, met a Night –
    We talked between the Rooms –
    Until the Moss had reached our lips –
    And covered up – our names "

28. The above poem, "I Died for Beauty" by Emily Dickinson, can best be summarized as which of the following?
    a. Companionship yielding to the coldness of death
    b. Failure to reach one's goals in life
    c. Two lovers who are laid to rest side by side
    d. A neglected cemetery
    e. A longing to live life over again

Question 29 pertains to the following passage:
    "This is God's curse on slavery!—a bitter, bitter, most accursed thing!—a curse to the master
    and a curse to the slave! I was a fool to think I could make anything good out of such a
    deadly evil."

29. The above quote is from which of the following works?
    a. Frederick Douglass' "The Heroic Slave"
    b. Augustus Baldwin Longstreet's "Georgia Scenes, Characters, Incidents, Etc"
    c. Harriet Beecher Stowe's "Uncle Tom's Cabin"
    d. William Wells Brown's "The Escape or, A Leap for Freedom"
    e. James Russell Lowell's "The Present Crisis"

30. "Yarns Spun by a Nat'ral Born Durn'd Fool" is a partial title attributed to which of the following fictional characters?
    a. Tom Sawyer
    b. Ichabod Crane
    c. Huckleberry Finn
    d. Captain Boomer
    e. Sut Lovingood

Question 31 pertains to the following passage:
    "TELL me not, in mournful numbers,
    Life is but an empty dream! —
    For the soul is dead that slumbers,
    And things are not what they seem.
    Life is real! Life is earnest!
    And the grave is not its goal;
    Dust thou art, to dust returnest,
    Was not spoken of the soul."

31. The above two passages are from which poem?
    a. Ralph Waldo Emerson's "Ode to Beauty"
    b. Walt Whitman's "A Clear Midnight"
    c. Emily Dickinson's "I have no life but this"
    d. Henry Wadsworth Longfellow's "A Psalm of Life"
    e. Edgar Allan Poe's "The Happiest Day"

32. What is the main theme of Edgar Allan Poe's "Masque of the Red Death"?
    a. How one will die remains a mystery throughout life
    b. No man or woman can escape death
    c. Man's will to live is more powerful than disease
    d. Live every day as if it were your last
    e. People continue to wear masks in death as they do in life

Question 33 pertains to the following passage:
> "No man for any considerable period can wear one face to himself and another to the multitude, without finally getting bewildered as to which may be the true."

33. The above quote is from which of the following works?
    a. Nathaniel Hawthorne's "The Scarlet Letter"
    b. Ralph Waldo Emerson's "Self-Reliance"
    c. Herman Melville's "Moby Dick"
    d James Fenimore Cooper's "Last of the Mohicans"
    e. Mark Twain's "How to Tell a Story"

Questions 34-35 refer to the following passage:
> "Helen, thy beauty is to me
> Like those Nicean barks of yore,
> That gently, o'er a perfumed sea,
> The weary, wayworn wanderer bore
> To his own native shore."

34. Who is Helen in the above passage from Edgar Allan Poe's "To Helen"?
    a. The speaker's wife
    b. A woman in a painting
    c. Helen of Troy in Greek mythology
    d. The speaker's deceased lover
    e. The ocean

Question 35 pertains to the following passage:
> "On desperate seas long wont to roam,
> Thy hyacinth hair, thy classic face,
> Thy Naiad airs have brought me home
> To the glory that was Greece
> And the grandeur that was Rome."

35. What do glory and grandeur represent, respectively, in the above passage?
    a. Victorious battles and fame
    b. Political power and wealth
    c. Popularity in the world and respectability
    d. Cultural significance and enormity of size and scale
    e. Religious faith and size of army

Question 36 pertains to the following passage:
    "In the bosom of one of those spacious coves which indent the eastern shore of the Hudson, at that broad expansion of the river denominated by the ancient Dutch navigators the Tappan Zee, and where they always prudently shortened sail and implored the protection of St. Nicholas when they crossed, there lies a small market town or rural port, which by some is called Greensburgh, but which is more generally and properly known by the name of Tarry Town."

36. The above passage is from which of the following works?
    a. Nathaniel Hawthorne's "The Canterbury Pilgrims"
    b. Henry David Thoreau's "Walden"
    c. Washington Irving's "The Legend of Sleepy Hollow"
    d. Edgar Allan Poe's "The Tell-tale Heart"
    e. T.B. Thorpe's "The Big Bear of Arkansas"

Question 37 pertains to the following passage:
    "So fanciful, so savage, nought cares he
    For number or proportion. Mockingly,
    On coop or kennel he hangs Parian wreaths;
    A swan-like form invests the hidden thorn;
    Fills up the farmer's lane from wall to wall,
    Maugre the farmer's sighs; and at the gate
    A tapering turret overtops the work.
    And when his hours are numbered, and the world
    Is all his own, retiring, as he were not,
    Leaves, when the sun appears, astonished Art
    To mimic in slow structures, stone by stone,
    Built in an age, the mad wind's night-work,
    The frolic architecture of the snow."

37. In the above passage from Ralph Waldo Emerson's "The Snow-Storm," which of the following does NOT characterize the snowstorm?
    a. A force that leaves destruction in its wake
    b. Something with which man cannot compete
    c. A work of art
    d. A force that does as it pleases
    e. Fierce yet beautiful

"Hope is the thing with feathers—
That perches in the soul—
And sings the tune without the words—
And never stops—at all—

And sweetest—in the Gale—is heard—
And sore must be the storm—
That could abash the little Bird
That kept so many warm—

I've heard it in the 100hilliest land—
And on the strangest Sea—
Yet, never, in Extremity,
It asked a crumb—of Me."

38. In Emily Dickinson's poem above, "Hope is a Thing with Feathers," which statement best summarizes what the speaker believes about hope?
   a. Hope is something to cling to in stormy times
   b. Hope exists but is intangible
   c. Without our soul on which to perch, hope would not exist
   d. Like a bird, hope can fly out of reach
   e. Hope never ends as long as we let it fly and sing freely

39. Which of the following works written during the 1840s has been called "one of the great documents of the West"?
   a. "Desert Solitaire" by Edward Abbey
   b. "The Horse Swap" by Augustus Baldwin Longstreet
   c. "All the Pretty Horses" by Cormac McCarthy
   d. "The Oregon Trail" by Francis Parkman
   e. "The Marshes of Glynn" by Sidney Lanier

Question 40 pertains to the following passage:
"There comes Emerson first, whose rich words, every one,
   Are like gold nails in temples to hang trophies on,
   Whose prose is grand verse, while his verse, the Lord knows,
   Is some of it pr – No, 'tis not even prose;"

"Here's Cooper, who's written six volumes to show
   He's as good as a lord: well, let's grant that he's so;
   If a person prefer that description of praise,
   Why, a coronet's certainly cheaper than bays;"

40. Based on the above excerpts from James Russell Lowell's "A Fable for Critics," what is the literary device and rhyme scheme used by the author?
    a. A critical analysis in iambic pentameter
    b. A characterization in blank verse
    c. A metaphor in enclosed rhyme
    d. A satire of rhyming couplets
    e. Verbal irony in sonnet form

41. Which of the following depicts the lives and fates of characters living in the Bowery district of New York?
    a. Jack London's "The Call of the Wild"
    b. Stephen Crane's "Maggie: A Girl of the Streets"
    c. Sarah Orne Jewett's "Country of the Pointed Firs"
    d. Henry James' "The Portrait of a Lady"
    e. Bret Harte's "The Luck of Roaring Camp"

42. Which of the following works of William Vaughn Moody, set in the West, contains a climactic scene in Act I, followed by a dramatic fall and explanation?
    a. "The Masque of Judgment"
    b. "The Fire Bringer"
    c. "The Great Divide"
    d. "The Sabine Woman"
    e. "The Death of Eve"

Question 43 pertains to the following passage:
> "There would be no one to live for her during those coming years; she would live for herself. There would be no powerful will bending hers in that blind persistence with which men and women believe they have a right to impose a private will upon a fellow-creature."

43. The above passage about Mrs. Mallard and her sister Josephine is from which of the following works?
    a. "The Story of an Hour" by Kate Chopin
    b. "The White Heron" by Sarah Orne Jewett
    c. "Sketches of Southern Life" by Frances Ellen Watkins Harper
    d. "Life in the Iron Mills" by Rebecca Harding Davis
    e. "The Custom of the Country" by Edith Wharton

44. In Rebecca Harding Davis' "Life in the Iron Mills," the narrator keeps the statue made by the character "Hugh" after he
    a. Is fired from his job
    b. Commits suicide
    c. Is arrested for car theft
    d. Marries someone else
    e. Moves to West Virginia

Question 45 pertains to the following passage:
  "Some say the world will end in fire,
  Some say in ice.
  From what I've tasted of desire
  I hold with those who favor fire.
  But if it had to perish twice,
  I think I know enough of hate
  To say that for destruction ice
  Is also great
  And would suffice."

45. In the above poem, "Fire and Ice" by Robert Frost, fire and ice represent what, respectively, to the speaker?
    a. Hot and cold
    b. Hatred and forgiveness
    c. Passion and indifference
    d. Death and life
    e. Summer and winter

46. Henry James described which of his works as "the strange and sinister embroidered on the very type of the normal and easy"?
    a. "A Tragedy of Errors"
    b. "Daisy Miller"
    c. "The Portrait of a Lady"
    d. "The Ambassadors"
    e. "The Turn of the Screw"

47. "The Octopus," by Frank Norris, is based on which of the following historical events?
    a. The abolition of slavery
    b. The Mussel Slough Tragedy of 1880
    c. The opening of the Suez Canal
    d. Krakatoa volcano explosion
    e. The creation of Yellowstone National Park

48. "The Devil's Dictionary," by Ambrose Bierce, is which of the following?
    a. A poem about the subtleties of Satan's temptations
    b. An article about the double-speak of nineteenth-century politicians
    c. A satirical dictionary that reinterprets terms in the English language
    d. A novella about a book used by common people to cast spells
    e. A journal kept by the author to assist in his choice of words

Questions 49-50 pertain to the following passage:
   "Laugh, and the world laughs with you; Weep, and you weep alone"

49. The above lines are from which of the following?
    a. "Nothing Gold Can Stay" by Robert Frost
    b. "Songs for the People" by Frances Ellen Watkins Harper
    c. "The Mockingbird" by Sidney Lanier
    d. "Solitude" by Ella Wheeler Wilcox
    e. "Miniver Cheevy" by Edward Arlington Robinson

50. The above passage suggests what about laughter and tears?
    a. It is okay to laugh with others, but one should only cry in solitude
    b. People enjoy being around happiness but not sorrow
    c. Unlike laughter, sorrow is something the world knows little about
    d. Happiness is contagious but sadness is not
    e. Laughter cures the world's problems, and weeping cures one's individual soul

Question 51 pertains to the following passage:
   "Nothing in education is so astonishing as the amount of ignorance it accumulates in the form of inert facts."

51. The above quote comes from which of the following works?
    a. "The Education of Henry Adams" by Henry Adams
    b. "The Point of View" by Henry James
    c. "The Grandissimes: A Story of Creole Life" by George Washington Cable
    d. "An Exercise in Analysis" by Gertrude Stein
    e. "The Marrow of Tradition" by Charles W. Chesnutt

52. Which poet of Realism and Naturalism was dubbed "The Children's Poet"?
    a. Ella Wheeler Wilcox
    b. Eugene Field
    c. Richard Hovey
    d. Edith Warton
    e. Frances Ellen Watkins Harper

53. Henry James, William Dean Howells, and Mark Twain were which of the following?
    a. Naturalists
    b. Romantics
    c. Transcendentalists
    d. Modernists
    e. Realists

54. Which of the following is NOT a theme of Henry James' "Daisy Miller"?
    a. Aging gracefully
    b. Cultural differences between the Old World and New World
    c. When in Rome, do as the Romans do
    d. Societal prejudice
    e. Nonconformity

Question 55 pertains to the following passage:
> "We wear the mask that grins and lies,
> It hides our cheeks and shades our eyes,—
> This debt we pay to human guile;
> With torn and bleeding hearts we smile,
> And mouth with myriad subtleties.
> Why should the world be over-wise,
> In counting all our tears and sighs?
> Nay, let them only see us, while
> We wear the mask.
> We smile, but, O great Christ, our cries
> To thee from tortured souls arise.
> We sing, but oh the clay is vile
> Beneath our feet, and long the mile;
> But let the world dream otherwise,
> We wear the mask!"

55. Paul Laurence Dunbar's "We Wear the Mask" is about which of the following?
    a. The mask we wear to hide from God
    b. Justification for declaring war on others
    c. The phoniness of society in general
    d. Slaves hiding their feelings from their masters
    e. The burdens felt by those in power

Question 56 pertains to the following passage:
> "Within him, as he hurled himself forward, was born a love, a despairing fondness for this flag which was near him. It was a creation of beauty and invulnerability. It was a goddess, radiant, that bended its form with an imperious gesture to him. It was a woman, red and white, hating and loving, that called him with the voice of his hopes."

56. The above quote is from which of the following works?
    a. Hamlin Garland's "Under the Lion's Paw"
    b. Stephen Crane's "The Red Badge of Courage"
    c. Mark Twain's "The American Claimant"
    d. John Hay's "Castilian Days"
    e. Kate Chopin's "The Storm"

Questions 57-58 pertain to the following passage:

"In men whom men condemn as ill
I find so much of goodness still.
In men whom men pronounce divine
I find so much of sin and blot
I do not dare to draw a line
Between the two, where God has not."

57. The above poem was written by which of the following?
    a. Joaquin Miller
    b. Walt Whitman
    c. Eugene Field
    d. Ben King
    e. Stephen Crane

58. The author of the above poem was known as which of the following?
    a. The Poet of Philosophy
    b. The Poet of Nature
    c. The Gold Rush Poet
    d. The Poet of the Sierras
    e. The Poet of Politics

Question 59 pertains to the following passage:

"Miniver loved the Medici,
Albeit he had never seen one;
He would have sinned incessantly
Could he have been one.

Miniver cursed the commonplace
 And eyed a khaki suit with loathing;
He missed the mediaeval grace
 Of iron clothing."

59. The above passages from Edward Arlington Robinson's "Miniver Cheevy" best capture the contrast between what?
    a. Miniver's career ambitions and his actuality
    b. Traveling abroad and staying home
    c. Miniver's gilded dream and his tarnished reality
    d. Colonial America and modern day America
    e. Miniver's childhood and his adulthood

60. Making difficult, often life-changing choices is depicted in which of the following poems?
    a. Sidney Lanier's "The Battle of Lexington"
    b. Robert Frost's "The Road Not Taken"
    c. Edith Wharton's "The Other Two"
    d. Richard Hovey's "At the Crossroads"
    e. Ella Wheeler Wilcox's "Which Are You?"

61. Which "Great American Novel" is the quintessential work that captures the mood of the Jazz Age?
    a. William Faulkner's "The Evening Sun"
    b. Katherine Anne Porter's "Ship of Fools"
    c. T.S. Eliot's "The Wasteland"
    d. Ernest Hemingway's "The Sun Also Rises"
    e. F. Scott Fitzgerald's "The Great Gatsby"

62. What do the three male characters have in common in Eugene O'Neill's play, "Long Day's Journey into Night"?
    a. Their jobs require extensive travel
    b. They are devoutly religious
    c. They are alcoholics
    d. They never married
    e. They are planning a journey to California

Question 63 pertains to the following passage:
    "I would always rather not know. Then, no matter what can happen, it was not me that talked."

63. The above quote is from which of the following works?
    a. Ernest Hemingway's "For Whom the Bell Tolls"
    b. Sherwood Anderson's "Winesburg, Ohio"
    c. Jean Toomer's "Blood Burning Moon"
    d. John Steinbeck's "Of Mice and Men"
    e. Willa Cather's "Paul's Case"

64. In William Faulkner's "A Rose for Emily," which of the following plays a key role in the story's plot development?
    a. A rose
    b. Arsenic
    c. A wedding ring
    d. Gasoline
    e. A bottle of red wine

Questions 65-66 pertains to the following passage:

> "Love is not all: It is not meat nor drink
> Nor slumber nor a roof against the rain,
> Nor yet a floating spar to men that sink
> and rise and sink and rise and sink again.
> Love cannot fill the thickened lung with breath
> Nor clean the blood, nor set the fractured bone;
> Yet many a man is making friends with death
> even as I speak, for lack of love alone.
> It well may be that in a difficult hour,
> pinned down by need and moaning for release
> or nagged by want past resolution's power,
> I might be driven to sell your love for peace,
> Or trade the memory of this night for food.
> It may well be. I do not think I would."

65. What type of poem is Edna St. Vincent Millay's "Love is Not All"?
    a. An ode
    b. A haiku
    c. A pastoral poem
    d. A cinquain
    e. A sonnet

66. In the above poem, what is the speaker's conclusion about love?
    a. She doesn't understand its importance to people
    b. She remains indifferent
    c. It happens only once in a lifetime
    d. It is worth more than anything in the world
    e. She would trade love for something better

67. "This is Just to Say," by William Carlos Williams, is a poem written as which of the following?
    a. A will
    b. A "to do" list
    c. A letter of confession
    d. A note on the refrigerator
    e. An instruction manual

68. Which of the following does NOT characterize the Modernist movement in American literature?
    a. The rejection of nineteenth-century traditions
    b. Influenced by rational philosophy
    c. Favoritism of free verse over metre for many poets
    d. Multiple point-of-view challenges tothe reader
    e. Replacement of Realism with Expressionism

69. Which of the following events had a profound influence on E. E. Cummings' work and led him in a new artistic direction?
    a. World War I
    b. His divorce from his second wife
    c. The untimely death of his father
    d. The bombing of Pearl Harbor
    e. His mother's illness

Question 70 pertains to the following passage:
    "Whirl up, sea—
    whirl your pointed pines,
    splash your great pines
    on our rocks,
    hurl your green over us,
    cover us with your pools of fir."

70. The above poem, "Oread" by H.D. (Hilda Doolittle), is an authentic example of which of the following:
    a. Imagism
    b. Symbolism
    c. Narrative
    d. Similes
    e. Didacticism

Question 71 pertains to the following passage:
    "For a second time there was no sign. Again no bridegroom and the priest in the house. She could not remember any other sorrow because this grief wiped them all away. Oh, no, there's nothing more cruel than this – I'll never forgive it. She stretched herself with a deep breath and blew out the light."

71. The above passage concludes which of the following works?
    a. "Death Comes for the Archbishop" by Willa Cather
    b. "The Jilting of Granny Weatherall" by Katherine Anne Porter
    c. "The Great Gatsby" by F. Scott Fitzgerald
    d. "A Grave" by Marianne Moore
    e. "Sister Carrie" by Theodore Dreiser

72. Which of the following best describes the subject of John Dos Passos' novel "Manhattan Transfer"?
    a. An anti-war novel about soldiers returning home to America
    b. Follows the lives of two people who commute via train into the city
    c. Reveals a transfer of political power from Chicago to Manhattan
    d. Depicts a city's struggle to embrace or risk being destroyed by modernity
    e. Follows the story of a music group struggling to make it in New York

73. Which of the following works was based on a notorious criminal case from the early 1900s, and has also been adapted into opera and film?
    a. Theodore Dreiser's "An American Tragedy"
    b. William Faulkner's "As I Lay Dying"
    c. Theodore Dreiser's "The Second Choice"
    d. F. Scott Fitzgerald's "Benjamin Button"
    e. Ernest Hemingway's "To Have and Have Not"

Question 74 pertains to the following passage:
        "In a station of the metro
        The apparition of these faces in the crowd;
        Petals on a wet, black bough."

74. "In a Station of the Metro," by Ezra Pound, is NOT considered to be which of the following?
    a. A leading poem of the Imagist tradition.
    b. An exercise in Realism
    c. Of Japanese haiku style
    d. A use of economy of language
    e. A break from the pentameter

Question 75 pertains to the following passage:
        "Fast rode the knight
        With spurs, hot and reeking,
        Ever waving an eager sword,
        "To save my lady!"
        Fast rode the knight,
        And leaped from saddle to war.
        Men of steel flickered and gleamed
        Like riot of silver lights,
        And the gold of the knight's good banner
        Still waved on a castle wall.
        . . . . .
        A horse,
        Blowing, staggering, bloody thing,
        Forgotten at foot of castle wall.
        A horse
        Dead at foot of castle wall."

75. What is the moral of Stephen Crane's "Fast Rode the Knight"?
    a. Even successful battles render casualties
    b. Horses were the only means of transport in battle
    c. Remember those who helped you achieve success
    d. Defending another requires sacrifice
    e. The horse was mortally wounded in battle

Question 76 pertains to the following passage:

> "maggie and milly and molly and may
> went down to the beach(to play one day)
>
> and maggie discovered a shell that sang
> so sweetly she couldn't remember her troubles, and
>
> milly befriended a stranded star
> whose rays five languid fingers were;
>
> and molly was chased by a horrible thing
> which raced sideways while blowing bubbles; and
>
> may came home with a smooth round stone
> as small as a world and as large as alone.
>
> For whatever we lose (like a you or a me)
> it's always ourselves we find in the sea"

76. In E. E. Cummings' poem "Maggie and Milly and Molly and May," the main theme is which of the following?
    a. A search for the self or identity
    b. The vastness of the beach compared to the smallness of a child
    c. The many treasures a beach holds
    d. The diversity of personal preference
    e. Frightening things can exist in beautiful settings

Question 77 pertains to the following passage:

"I walk down the garden paths,
And all the daffodils
Are blowing, and the bright blue squills.
I walk down the patterned garden-paths
In my stiff, brocaded gown.
With my powdered hair and jewelled fan,
I too am a rare
Pattern. As I wander down
The garden paths."

"In a month he would have been my husband.
In a month, here, underneath this lime,
We would have broke the pattern;
He for me, and I for him,
He as Colonel, I as Lady,
On this shady seat.
He had a whim
That sunlight carried blessing.
And I answered, "It shall be as you have said."
Now he is dead."

77. Based on the above excerpts, the pattern referred to in Amy Lowell's poem "Patterns" is which of the following?
    a. The landscaping of the garden
    b. An arranged marriage
    c. The wardrobe of the speaker
    d. Rules and expectations of Victorian society
    e. The day's schedule

78. Which of the following poems depicts an act of racial discrimination against a young boy that leaves a permanent impression in the boy's mind?
    a. "Mother to Son" by Langston Hughes
    b. "Incident" by Countee Cullen
    c. "There is Confusion" by Jessie Redmon Fauset
    d. "Strong Men" by Sterling A. Brown
    e. "Blood Burning Moon" by Jean Toomer

79. Which of the following is NOT a character in Ernest Hemingway's "A Farewell to Arms"?
    a. Frederic Henry
    b. Catherine Barkley
    c. Nick Carraway
    d. The Priest
    e. Rinaldi

80. Which of the following best summarizes the plot of William Faulkner's "The Sound and the Fury"?
    a. The treatment of slaves in the South
    b. The decline of the once noble Compson family
    c. The Compson family's accrual of wealth through land ownership
    d. A son's adjustment to normal life after fighting in the Civil War
    e. The consequences of sibling rivalry

Questions 81-82 pertains to the following passage:
    "This is the way the world ends.
    This is the way the world ends.
    This is the way the world ends.
    Not with a bang but a whimper."

81. The above stanza is from which of the following poems?
    a. Sherwood Anderson's "I Want to Know Why"
    b. Ezra Pound's "Cantos"
    c. Robert Frost's "Birches"
    d. Simon Ortiz's "Hunger in New York City"
    e. T.S. Eliot's "The Hollow Men"

82. To which historic event is the last line of the above stanza referring?
    a. The Great Depression
    b. The end of the Gunpowder Plot
    c. The Scopes "Monkey Trial"
    d. Ratification of the 19th amendment to the Constitution
    e. The death of communist leader Vladimir Lenin

83. Which of the following authors was NOT considered to be one of the Lost Generation?
    a. Ernest Hemingway
    b. Gertrude Stein
    c. John Dos Passos
    d. Langston Hughes
    e. F. Scott Fitzgerald

84. Philip Marlowe is the protagonist from the works of which author's private detective stories?
    a. Raymond Chandler
    b. Dashiell Hammet
    c. Eugene O'Neill
    d. Margery Allingham
    e. Agatha Christie

Question 85 pertains to the following passage:

"While this America settles in the mould of its vulgarity, heavily thickening

to empire / And protest, only a bubble in the molten mass, pops and sighs out, and the

mass hardens, / I sadly smiling remember that the flower fades to make fruit, the fruit rots

to make earth. / Out of the mother; and through the spring exultances, ripeness and deca-

dence; and home to the mother.

You making haste haste on decay: not blameworthy; life is good, be it stubbornly long or suddenly / A mortal splendor: meteors are not needed less than mountains: shine, perishing republic. / But for my children, I would have them keep their distance from the thickening center; corruption / Never has been compulsory, when the cities lie at the monster's feet there are left the mountains. / And boys, be in nothing so moderate as in love of man, a clever servant, insufferable master. / There is the trap that catches noblest spirits, that caught— they say—God, when he walked on earth."

85. The above poem, "Shine, Perishing Republic" by Robinson Jeffers, expresses which philosophy that he would continue to explore throughout his career?
    a. Patriotism
    b. Inhumanism
    c. Communism
    d. Separatism
    e. Scientology

86. Who was one of the greatest influences on the literary career of Sylvia Plath?
    a. Her best friend
    b. Her brother
    c. Her college English professor
    d. Her husband
    e. Her father

87. Called "one of the best American wartime novels" by many critics, which of the following works, based on the author's own experience in World War II, portrays the heroic struggle of soldiers to retain their dignity amidst the horrors of war?
    a. Roger McGough's "A Square Dance"
    b. R.L. Barth's "A Letter to the Dead"
    c. Norman Mailer's "The Naked and the Dead"
    d. Richard Wright's "Eight Men"
    e. Flannery O'Connor's "The Life You Save May Be Your Own"

88. The title for Lorraine Hansberry's play "A Raisin in the Sun" comes from which of the following works?

    a."Sermons and Blues" by James Baldwin

    b. "A Dream Deferred" by Langston Hughes

    c. "Seize the Day" by Saul Bellow

    d. "The Jewbird" by Bernard Malamud

    e. "Dream Song 1" by John Berryman

89. Which of the following is NOT a character from Tennessee Williams' "A Streetcar Named Desire"?

    a. Stanley Kowalski

    b. Blanche DuBois

    c. Mitch

    d. Stella Kowalski

    e Amanda Wingfield

90. Arthur Miller's play "The Crucible," based on events that led to the Salem Witch Trials, was in response to which of the following?

    a. NASA's preparation to send man to the moon

    b. The assassination of John F. Kennedy

    c. Martin Luther King's "I Have a Dream" speech

    d. The practice of McCarthyism

    e. The bombing raids on North Vietnam

91. Eudora Welty's short story "A Worn Path" could best be described as which of the following?

    a. An account of the beauty of the Natchez Trace

    b. A tale of undying love and devotion

    c. A horror story about a rabid dog

    d. A frightful tale of a woman's encounter with a hunter

    e. A romance

92. Which of the following plays depicts a family's dark secret?

    a. Sam Shepard's "Buried Child"

    b. Arthur Miller's "Death of a Salesman"

    c. Tennessee Williams' "The Glass Menagerie"

    d. Harold Pinter's "The Birthday Party"

    e. Edward Albee's "The Sandbox"

93. Belligerence, drunkenness, and the intermingling of illusion and reality are present throughout which of the following works?

    a. Harper Lee's "To Kill a Mockingbird"

    b. John Cheever's "The Swimmer"

    c. Tennessee Williams' "Cat on a Hot Tin Roof"

    d. Ralph Ellison's "Invisible Man"

    e. Edward Albee's "Who's Afraid of Virginia Woolf?"

Question 94 pertains to the following passage:

"Hog Butcher for the World / Tool Maker, Stacker of Wheat / Player with Railroads and the Nation's Freight Handler, / Stormy, Husky, Brawling, / City of the Big Shoulders."

94. The above description by Carl Sandburg refers to which American city?
   a. Detroit
   b. Chicago
   c. Milwaukee
   d. New York City
   e. Cincinnati

Question 95 pertains to the following passage:

"I wake to sleep, and take my waking slow.
I feel my fate in what I cannot fear.
I learn by going where I have to go."

95. The first and third lines in the above passage from Theodore Roethke's "The Waking" are examples of which literary device?
   a. Paradox
   b. Metaphor
   c. Hyperbole
   d. Simile
   e. Parallelism

96. "Having a Coke with You" and "Meditations in an Emergency" are poems that exemplified Frank O'Hara's
   a. Focus on things most others do not notice
   b. Preference for strict metre in poetry
   c. Observations on what was happening with him at the moment
   d. Use of hyperbole
   e. Views of other people

Question 97 pertains to the following passage:

"The surface / Of the mirror being convex, the distance increases / Significantly."
"They seek and cannot find the meaning in music, / We see only postures of the dream."

- 115 -

97. Based on the above lines from John Ashbery's "Self-Portrait in a Convex Mirror," the speaker believes which of the following to be true?
    a. Words, like paintings, sometimes prove inadequate in their expression
    b. Even mirror images can be deceptive
    c. There is often no real meaning behind portraits and prose
    d. We see only what we choose to see in art
    e. There is too much distance between artist and art for them to ever be one

Question 98 pertains to the following passage:
    "Every year without knowing it I have passed the day
    When the last fires will wave to me
    And the silence will set out
    Tireless traveler
    Like the beam of a lightless star

    Then I will no longer
    Find myself in life as in a strange garment
    Surprised at the earth
    And the love of one woman
    And the shamelessness of men
    As today writing after three days of rain
    Hearing the wren sing and the falling cease
    And bowing not knowing to what"

98. W.S. Merwin's "For the Anniversary of My Death" depicts which of the following?
    a. A traveler stopping to gaze at a cemetery
    b. A vision of heaven and hell
    c. The fears of a man on his deathbed
    d. A mourning of oneself upon his own death
    e. A dream on the anniversary of a loved one's death

Questions 99-100 pertain to the following passage:
    "It was times like these when I thought my father, who hated guns and had never been to any wars, was the bravest man who ever lived."

99. What is the name of the character who spoke the above words?
    a. Edna Pontellier
    b. Scout Finch
    c. Sethe
    d. Blanche DuBois
    e. Narrator

100. Name the work and author the quote above is taken from.
    a. "The Awakening" by Kate Chopin
    b. "Invisible Man" by Ralph Ellison
    c. "To Kill a Mockingbird" by Harper Lee
    d. "A Streetcar Named Desire" by Tennessee Williams
    e. "Beloved" by Toni Morrison

Answers and Explanations

1. D	21. C	41. B	61. E	81. E
2. C	22. A	42. C	62. C	82. B
3. D	23. D	43. A	63. A	83. D
4. E	24. B	44. B	64. B	84. A
5. A	25. E	45. C	65. E	85. B
6. C	26. D	46. E	66. D	86. E
7. B	27. B	47. B	67. D	87. C
8. B	28. A	48. C	68. B	88. B
9. D	29. C	49. D	69. C	89. E
10. A	30. E	50. B	70. A	90. D
11. E	31. D	51. A	71. B	91. B
12. B	32. B	52. B	72. D	92. A
13. A	33. A	53. E	73. A	93. E
14. C	34. C	54. A	74. B	94. B
15. D	35. D	55. D	75. C	95. A
16. E	36. C	56. B	76. A	96. C
17. B	37. A	57. A	77. D	97. A
18. C	38. E	58. D	78. B	98. D
19. D	39. D	59. C	79. C	99. B
20. B	40. D	60. B	80. B	100. C

1. D: "A Funeral Poem on the Death of C.E." was written by Phillis Wheatley.

2. C: Borrowed from Jesus' Sermon on the Mount in the book of Matthew, John Winthrop introduced the phrase "city upon a hill" into early American literature to describe the community formed by the Puritan colonists, which was to be watched by the world.

3. D: Philip Freneau was sometimes called the "Poet of the American Revolution," having written a number of anti-British pieces before, during, and after the Revolutionary War.

4. E: Novels depicting regional dialect were prominent in the period of Realism.

5. A: A diary of a journey, "The Journal of Madam Knight" by Sarah Kemble Knight recounts the author's experiences during a trying journey. This passage details when her journey began and how far she would travel.

6. C: Natty Bumppo, a fictitious rugged "pioneer," was first introduced by Cooper in "Pioneers"; the character appears in all five of Cooper's works collectively titled "The Leatherstocking Tales."

7. B: A writer of satire as well as music and poetry, Francis Hopkinson, in "A Pretty Story," examines the contentious relationship between Great Britain and the colonies. It is often called the most important of his political writings.

8. B: Delivered March 23, 1775, this famous speech by Patrick Henry presented resolutions to raise a militia and to put Virginia in a posture of defense. "Give me liberty or give me death" were Henry's unforgettable closing words.

9. D: Bradstreet uses hyperbole in her description of love being "more than whole mines of gold" or "all the riches that the East doth hold." In the line "My love is such that rivers cannot quench," the poet uses metaphor to compare her love to a thirst that nothing can quench.

10. A: Michael Wigglesworth's "The Day of Doom" is a poetical description of the Great and Last Judgment. The first excerpt describes the atmosphere of calm the evening before the "storm" of Judgment Day.

11. E: In this work, Loyalist Joseph Galloway pled the case for restitution from the Crown in England.

12. B: The first excerpt from Edward Taylor's "Upon a Wasp Chilled with Cold" describes a wasp in vivid detail.

13. A: In the second excerpt, the speaker pleads with God to clear his sight so that he can see His divinity through the wasp.

14. C: Ebenezer Cooke's "The Sot-Weed Factor" describes the outlandish food and eating habits, the excessive drinking and fighting, and the admixture of law with violence, as well as the intellectual poverty and lack of education, that characterized this time.

15. D: In Anne Bradstreet's "Upon the Burning of Our House," the use of the word "fire" alludes to the day of judgment, and she is acknowledging here that her goal is to be prepared.

16. E: Washington Irving's "Rip Van Winkle" is framed by commentary from an unknown narrator. In the first passage, this narrator explains the story's origin to the reader.

17. B: Nathaniel Hawthorne's "The Scarlet Letter," which contrasts Puritan morality with individualism, is an example of Transcendentalism.

18. C: Tom Canty is a character in Mark Twain's "The Prince and the Pauper."

19. D: The word "house" in Emily Dickinson's poem "Because I Could Not Stop for Death" refers to the tomb in which she will reside for eternity.

20. B: "The Philosophy of Composition" was written by Edgar Allan Poe following "The Raven," which he claimed to have written very methodically.

21. C: Romanticism is the exaltation of the senses and emotions over reason and intellect. Answer (A) describes Naturalism; answer (B) describes Puritanism; answer (D) describes Realism; and answer (E) describes Transcendentalism.

22. A: In Walt Whitman's "A Noiseless Patient Spider," the poet uses alliteration in the third line of the first stanza by including the words "vacant" and "vast, " and in line 4 by the use of "forth " and the word "filament" three successive times.

23. D: In the second stanza, the poet uses metaphor to compare the speaker in the poem to a spider, the speaker's bond to a bridge, attachment to an anchor, and exploration to a gossamer thread.

24. B: Betrayal of a friend was not a theme in Herman Melville's "Moby Dick."

25. E: Ralph Waldo Emerson's definition of genius begins in the fourth line of "Self-Reliance."

26. D: "The Maypole of Merry Mount" by Nathaniel Hawthorne depicts the conflict and social tensions between the Merry Mount colonists and the Puritans.

27. B: Henry David Thoreau's "Walden" was an experiment in social isolation, therefore not an exercise in understanding the characteristics of others.

28. A: The kinship established between two deceased persons laid to rest side by side is gradually lost as overgrowth silences their speech and hides their identities.

29. C: This quote is from Chapter 5 of Harriet Beecher Stowe's "Uncle Tom's Cabin."

30. E: The full title is "Sut Lovingood: Yarns Spun by a 'Nat'ral Born Durn'd Fool,'" by George Washington Harris.

31. D: These are the first two passages from Henry Wadsworth Long fellow's "A Psalm of Life."

32. B: The theme of Edgar Allan Poe's "Masque of the Red Death" is that, although men and women do all they can to postpone death; no one can ultimately escape it.

33. A: The quote is from Chapter 20, "The Minister in a Maze," of Nathaniel Hawthorne's "The Scarlet Letter."

34. C: Poe is alluding to Helen of Troy, the daughter of the god Zeus in Greek mythology. In literature she is often referred to as the most beautiful woman who ever lived.

35. D: In these two frequently quoted lines, "glory" refers to Greece's numerous cultural contributions to the world and "grandeur" refers to the sheer size, scale, and immensity of Rome and its structures.

36. C: This passage begins Washington Irving's "The Legend of Sleepy Hollow."

37. A: Ralph Waldo Emerson's "The Snow-Storm" depicts the snowstorm's beauty, art, power, and ability to do as it pleases, focusing on the beauty it leaves behind rather than the destruction it causes.

38. E: In Emily Dickinson's "Hope is a thing with feathers," hope is described in a positive light, as something that is never-ending, freely given, and never asks for anything in return.

39. D: Francis Parkman's "The Oregon Trail" sets down for posterity what Parkman observed on his trip to the Rocky Mountains. Few travelers wrote much about the country beyond the Mississippi as early as the 1840s, making it an important account of this region.

40. D: A light-hearted assault on the nineteenth-century American literary scene, James Russell Lowell's "A Fable for Critics" is a satire in rhyming couplets.

41. B: Stephen Crane's "Maggie: A Girl of the Streets" depicts Maggie and her family, citizens of New York's Bowery district, but it could be about anyone who lived through hard times in that part of the city.

42. C: William Vaughn Moody's "The Great Divide" reaches its climax in the middle of the first act when Ruth Jordan agrees to marry Stephen Ghent.

43. A: The passage comes from Kate Chopin's "The Story of an Hour" as Mrs. Mallard nears death.

44. B: After a series of bad decisions, Hugh is arrested and put in jail, where he commits suicide by slitting his wrists. Hugh's decline was prompted by critical comments about a statue of a woman he had made, and after his death the narrator keeps the statue.

45. C: In "Fire and Ice" by Robert Frost, the speaker initially speculates that the end of the world will be caused by fire—or too much passion. But in contemplating the

possibility of it perishing a second time, he can see how ice—or indifference—might also be a justified cause.

46. E: Henry James' "The Turn of the Screw" is an ambiguous ghost story in which the ghosts are depicted as extensions of everyday reality.

47. B: Based on the Mussel Slough Tragedy of 1880, Frank Norris' "The Octopus" depicts the conflict between wheat farmers in California's San Joaquin Valley and the Pacific and Southwestern Railroad.

48. C: Ambrose Bierce's "The Devil's Dictionary" earned him the nickname the "laughing devil of San Francisco" because it is a comic dictionary containing satirical definitions of English language terms.

49. D: "Solitude," published by Ella Wheeler Cox in 1883, begins with "Laugh, and the world laughs with you; Weep, and you weep alone."

50. B: The passage expresses the idea that people enjoy being around those who are happy and joyful, but distance themselves from those who are sad, as sadness is more difficult to be around.

51. A: The quote is from Henry Adams' "The Education of Henry Adams."

52. B: Eugene Field was dubbed "The Children's Poet" because he was one of the few poets who wrote only children's poetry.

53. E: Henry James, William Dean Howells, and Mark Twain were writers of the Realist movement. The Realists attempted to show some deeper meaning in the lives of ordinary characters and believed that external forces could limit human free will.

54. A: Aging gracefully is not a theme of Henry James' "Daisy Miller."

55. D: In Paul Laurence Dunbar's "We Wear the Mask," the "we" refers to slaves who, although oppressed and living lives of hardship and struggle, were expected to appear carefree and happy.

56. B: The quote is from Chapter 19 of Stephen Crane's "The Red Badge of Courage."

57. A: This is the poem "Byron," by Joaquin Miller.

58. D: Miller was called the "Poet of the Sierras" because of his famous work "Songs of the Sierras."

59. C: In Edward Arlington Robinson's "Miniver Cheevy," Miniver longs for the grandeur and romance of medieval times and therefore loathes the culture in which he actually lives.

60. B: In his poem "The Road Not Taken," Robert Frost depicts a traveler having to make a tough choice at a fork in the road and ultimately choosing the less traveled path.

61. E: Often called "The Great American Novel," F. Scott Fitzgerald's "The Great Gatsby" is about an era Fitzgerald himself dubbed "The Jazz Age."

62. C: Eugene O'Neill's "Long Day's Journey into Night," a play about addiction and the resulting family dysfunction, centers on three male characters, who are all alcoholics. Additionally, one of the female characters, Mary Cavan Tyrone, is addicted to morphine.

63. A: The quote is from Chapter 1 of Ernest Hemingway's "For Whom the Bell Tolls."

64. B: In William Faulkner's "A Rose for Emily," Emily purchases arsenic, which she uses to poison her beau, Homer Barron.

65. E: Edna St. Vincent Millay's "Love is Not All" is a sonnet, a verse form that always contains fourteen lines.

66. D: Although the speaker begins by focusing on what love is not, she ultimately concludes that she would not trade it for anything.

67. D: William Carlos' Williams' "This is Just to Say" appears to the reader like a piece of found poetry, a note left on the refrigerator, asking forgiveness for eating the plums.

68. B: The movement influenced by rational philosophy was Realism, not Modernism.

69. C: E.E. Cummings' work was directly impacted by the death of his father, who was killed when a train struck his car.

70. A: Like Richard Aldington and Ezra Pound, H.D. was an Imagist poet. "Oread" provides a true example of this type of poetry.

71. B: The quote is from Katherine Anne Porter's "The Jilting of Granny Weatherall," in which Granny is jilted two times. The first time occurs on her wedding day; nearing death, the "bridegroom" she is expecting again does not appear to give her a sign of the afterlife.

72. D: An exercise in stream of consciousness technique, John Dos Passos' "Manhattan Transfer" reveals the lives and struggles of wealthy powerbrokers as well as poor immigrants, all trying to make it in an ever-growing, unfeeling metropolis.

73. A: Theodore Dreiser's "An American Tragedy" is based on Chester Gillette's murder of Grace Brown. Gillette was sentenced to death for the crime, although he claimed Brown's death was an accident. The novel was adapted into an opera in 2005 and it also inspired the film "A Place in the Sun."

74. B: Ezra Pound's poem "In a Station of the Metro" is characteristic of Modernism and Imagism. It does not express Realism.

75. C: Stephen Crane's "Fast Rode the Knight" depicts the gallantry of the knights at the expense of the lives of their horses, who are forgotten as soon as the battle is won. It serves to remind the reader that those who are critical to one's success should not be forgotten.

76. A: E.E. Cummings' poem "maggie and milly and molly and may" reveals how four girls each find something at the sea that is quite unlike what the others find, thus highlighting each girl's unique identity.

77. D: In Amy Lowell's poem "Patterns," the word "pattern" refers to the rigidity of the rules and expectations of Victorian society, in which even the most intense emotions must be suppressed for propriety's sake.

78. B: In his poem "Incident," Countee Cullen recalls a trip to Baltimore from the point of view of an 8-year-old boy. Although the boy spends eight months in the city, the incident that makes the deepest impression on him is having been the target of a racial slur.

79. C: Nick Carraway is a character from F. Scott Fitzgerald's "The Great Gatsby."

80. B: William Faulkner's "The Sound and the Fury" follows the decline of the Compsons, a once noble southern family, as they fall into financial ruin, lose their faith, and lose the town's respect, with some family members dying tragically.

81. E: The excerpt is the last stanza of T.S. Eliot's "The Hollow Men."

82. B: The last line of the stanza refers to the actual end of the Gunpowder Plot—not with its planned "bang," but with Guy Fawkes' whimper upon being captured.

83. D: Langston Hughes was one of the writers of the Harlem Renaissance movement.

84. A: Raymond Chandler's protagonist, Philip Marlow, became synonymous with "private detective," depicting style and attitudes now characteristic of the genre.

85. B: Robinson Jeffers' "Shine, Perishing Republic" reveals the author's' views on what he saw as inhumanism, the country's underlying trend toward dictatorship and corruption, and the coming extinction of the human race.

86. E: Sylvia Plath's father died when she was just eight years old, inspiring her famous poems "Daddy" and "Electra on Azalea Path."

87. C: Norman Mailer's "The Naked and the Dead," based on the author's military service in World War II, was named one of Modern Library's "100 Best English-Language Novels of the 20th Century." It focuses on a 14-man infantry platoon's struggle to survive and find meaning in their lives amidst war.

88. B: The title for Lorraine Hansberry's "A Raisin in the Sun" comes from Langston Hughes' poem "A Dream Deferred," which includes the lines, "What happens to a dream deferred? Does it dry up like a raisin in the sun?"

89. E: Amanda Wingfield is a character in Tennessee Williams' play "The Glass Menagerie."

90. D: Arthur Miller's "The Crucible" was written in response to McCarthyism, the name often applied to the U.S. government's active hunt for communists during the 1950s, led by Wisconsin senator Joseph McCarthy.

91. B: Eudora Welty's "A Worn Path," the story of a grandmother who faces the dangers of a journey alone to obtain medication for her sick grandson, is at its core a tale of love and devotion.

92. A: Sam Shepard's "Buried Child" centers on a Midwestern American family with a dark secret: A baby, the result of an act of incest, was drowned and buried in the field behind their farmhouse.

93. E: In Edward Albee's "Who's Afraid of Virginia Woolf?" married couple George and Martha get drunk and become verbally and physically abusive toward one another in front of guests and, throughout the play, refer to a son who does not really exist.

94. B: The passage is from Carl Sandburg's poem "Chicago" and is a famous description of the title city.

95. A: In Theodore Roethke's "The Waking," "waking to sleep" and "learning by going where you have to go" are both paradoxes, as they contain two diametrically opposed ideas in one line.

96. C: Frank O'Hara was a poet known for writing primarily autobiographical poems based on observations he was making at the moment. Much of his poetry was written "impromptu," seemingly dashed off during meetings, while eating lunch, etc.

97. A: These lines from John Ashbery's "Self-Portrait in a Convex Mirror" suggest that, like brushstrokes in a painting, words are not always sufficient for rendering experience.

98. D: W.S. Merwin's "For the Anniversary of My Death" consists primarily in the author mourning himself upon his own death, and reflecting on the experience of dying and on the afterlife.

99. B: These words are spoken by the character Scout Finch.

100. C: The quote is from Chapter 11 in Harper Lee's "To Kill a Mockingbird."

Secret Key #1 - Time is Your Greatest Enemy

Pace Yourself

Wear a watch. At the beginning of the test, check the time (or start a chronometer on your watch to count the minutes), and check the time after every few questions to make sure you are "on schedule."

If you are forced to speed up, do it efficiently. Usually one or more answer choices can be eliminated without too much difficulty. Above all, don't panic. Don't speed up and just begin guessing at random choices. By pacing yourself, and continually monitoring your progress against your watch, you will always know exactly how far ahead or behind you are with your available time. If you find that you are one minute behind on the test, don't skip one question without spending any time on it, just to catch back up. Take 15 fewer seconds on the next four questions, and after four questions you'll have caught back up. Once you catch back up, you can continue working each problem at your normal pace.

Furthermore, don't dwell on the problems that you were rushed on. If a problem was taking up too much time and you made a hurried guess, it must be difficult. The difficult questions are the ones you are most likely to miss anyway, so it isn't a big loss. It is better to end with more time than you need than to run out of time.

Lastly, sometimes it is beneficial to slow down if you are constantly getting ahead of time. You are always more likely to catch a careless mistake by working more slowly than quickly, and among very high-scoring test takers (those who are likely to have lots of time left over), careless errors affect the score more than mastery of material.

Secret Key #2 - Guessing is not Guesswork

You probably know that guessing is a good idea. Unlike other standardized tests, there is no penalty for getting a wrong answer. Even if you have no idea about a question, you still have a 20-25% chance of getting it right.

Most test takers do not understand the impact that proper guessing can have on their score. Unless you score extremely high, guessing will significantly contribute to your final score.

Monkeys Take the Test

What most test takers don't realize is that to insure that 20-25% chance, you have to guess randomly. If you put 20 monkeys in a room to take this test, assuming they answered once per question and behaved themselves, on average they would get 20-25% of the questions correct. Put 20 test takers in the room, and the average will be much lower among guessed questions. Why?

1. The test writers intentionally write deceptive answer choices that "look" right. A test taker has no idea about a question, so he picks the "best looking" answer, which is often wrong. The monkey has no idea what looks good and what doesn't, so it will consistently be right about 20-25% of the time.
2. Test takers will eliminate answer choices from the guessing pool based on a hunch or intuition. Simple but correct answers often get excluded, leaving a 0% chance of being correct. The monkey has no clue, and often gets lucky with the best choice.

This is why the process of elimination endorsed by most test courses is flawed and detrimental to your performance. Test takers don't guess; they make an ignorant stab in the dark that is usually worse than random.

$5 Challenge

Let me introduce one of the most valuable ideas of this course—the $5 challenge:

You only mark your "best guess" if you are willing to bet $5 on it.
You only eliminate choices from guessing if you are willing to bet $5 on it.

Why $5? Five dollars is an amount of money that is small yet not insignificant, and can really add up fast (20 questions could cost you $100). Likewise, each answer choice on one question of the test will have a small impact on your overall score, but it can really add up to a lot of points in the end.

The process of elimination IS valuable. The following shows your chance of guessing it right:

If you eliminate wrong answer choices until only this many remain:	Chance of getting it correct:
1	100%
2	50%
3	33%

However, if you accidentally eliminate the right answer or go on a hunch for an incorrect answer, your chances drop dramatically—to 0%. By guessing among all the answer choices, you are GUARANTEED to have a shot at the right answer.

That's why the $5 test is so valuable. If you give up the advantage and safety of a pure guess, it had better be worth the risk.

What we still haven't covered is how to be sure that whatever guess you make is truly random. Here's the easiest way:

Always pick the first answer choice among those remaining.

Such a technique means that you have decided, **before you see a single test question**, exactly how you are going to guess, and since the order of choices tells you nothing about which one is correct, this guessing technique is perfectly random.

This section is not meant to scare you away from making educated guesses or eliminating choices; you just need to define when a choice is worth eliminating. The $5 test, along with a pre-defined random guessing strategy, is the best way to make sure you reap all of the benefits of guessing.

Secret Key #3 - Practice Smarter, Not Harder

Many test takers delay the test preparation process because they dread the awful amounts of practice time they think necessary to succeed on the test. We have refined an effective method that will take you only a fraction of the time.

There are a number of "obstacles" in the path to success. Among these are answering questions, finishing in time, and mastering test-taking strategies. All must be executed on the day of the test at peak performance, or your score will suffer. The test is a mental marathon that has a large impact on your future.

Just like a marathon runner, it is important to work your way up to the full challenge. So first you just worry about questions, and then time, and finally strategy:

Success Strategy

1. Find a good source for practice tests.
2. If you are willing to make a larger time investment, consider using more than one study guide. Often the different approaches of multiple authors will help you "get" difficult concepts.
3. Take a practice test with no time constraints, with all study helps, "open book." Take your time with questions and focus on applying strategies.
4. Take a practice test with time constraints, with all guides, "open book."
5. Take a final practice test without open material and with time limits.

If you have time to take more practice tests, just repeat step 5. By gradually exposing yourself to the full rigors of the test environment, you will condition your mind to the stress of test day and maximize your success.

Secret Key #4 - Prepare, Don't Procrastinate

Let me state an obvious fact: if you take the test three times, you will probably get three different scores. This is due to the way you feel on test day, the level of preparedness you have, and the version of the test you see. Despite the test writers' claims to the contrary, some versions of the test WILL be easier for you than others.

Since your future depends so much on your score, you should maximize your chances of success. In order to maximize the likelihood of success, you've got to prepare in advance. This means taking practice tests and spending time learning the information and test taking strategies you will need to succeed.

Never go take the actual test as a "practice" test, expecting that you can just take it again if you need to. Take all the practice tests you can on your own, but when you go to take the official test, be prepared, be focused, and do your best the first time!

Secret Key #5 - Test Yourself

Everyone knows that time is money. There is no need to spend too much of your time or too little of your time preparing for the test. You should only spend as much of your precious time preparing as is necessary for you to get the score you need.

Once you have taken a practice test under real conditions of time constraints, then you will know if you are ready for the test or not.

If you have scored extremely high the first time that you take the practice test, then there is not much point in spending countless hours studying. You are already there.

Benchmark your abilities by retaking practice tests and seeing how much you have improved. Once you consistently score high enough to guarantee success, then you are ready.

If you have scored well below where you need, then knuckle down and begin studying in earnest. Check your improvement regularly through the use of practice tests under real conditions. Above all, don't worry, panic, or give up. The key is perseverance!

Then, when you go to take the test, remain confident and remember how well you did on the practice tests. If you can score high enough on a practice test, then you can do the same on the real thing.

General Strategies

The most important thing you can do is to ignore your fears and jump into the test immediately. Do not be overwhelmed by any strange-sounding terms. You have to jump into the test like jumping into a pool—all at once is the easiest way.

Make Predictions

As you read and understand the question, try to guess what the answer will be. Remember that several of the answer choices are wrong, and once you begin reading them, your mind will immediately become cluttered with answer choices designed to throw you off. Your mind is typically the most focused immediately after you have read the question and digested its contents. If you can, try to predict what the correct answer will be. You may be surprised at what you can predict.

Quickly scan the choices and see if your prediction is in the listed answer choices. If it is, then you can be quite confident that you have the right answer. It still won't hurt to check the other answer choices, but most of the time, you've got it!

Answer the Question

It may seem obvious to only pick answer choices that answer the question, but the test writers can create some excellent answer choices that are wrong. Don't pick an answer just because it sounds right, or you believe it to be true. It MUST answer the question. Once you've made your selection, always go back and check it against the question and make sure that you didn't misread the question and that the answer choice does answer the question posed.

Benchmark

After you read the first answer choice, decide if you think it sounds correct or not. If it doesn't, move on to the next answer choice. If it does, mentally mark that answer choice. This doesn't mean that you've definitely selected it as your answer choice, it just means that it's the best you've seen thus far. Go ahead and read the next choice. If the next choice is worse than the one you've already selected, keep going to the next answer choice. If the next choice is better than the choice you've already selected, mentally mark the new answer choice as your best guess.

The first answer choice that you select becomes your standard. Every other answer choice must be benchmarked against that standard. That choice is correct until proven otherwise by another answer choice beating it out. Once you've decided that no other answer choice seems as good, do one final check to ensure that your answer choice answers the question posed.

Valid Information

Don't discount any of the information provided in the question. Every piece of information may be necessary to determine the correct answer. None of the information in the question is there to throw you off (while the answer choices will certainly have information to throw you off). If two seemingly unrelated topics are discussed, don't ignore either. You can be confident there is a relationship, or it wouldn't be included in the question, and you are probably going to have to determine what is that relationship to find the answer.

Avoid "Fact Traps"

Don't get distracted by a choice that is factually true. Your search is for the answer that answers the question. Stay focused and don't fall for an answer that is true but irrelevant. Always go back to the question and make sure you're choosing an answer that actually answers the question and is not just a true statement. An answer can be factually correct, but it MUST answer the question asked. Additionally, two answers can both be seemingly correct, so be sure to read all of the answer choices, and make sure that you get the one that BEST answers the question.

Milk the Question

Some of the questions may throw you completely off. They might deal with a subject you have not been exposed to, or one that you haven't reviewed in years. While your lack of knowledge about the subject will be a hindrance, the question itself can give you many clues that will help you find the correct answer. Read the question carefully and look for clues. Watch particularly for adjectives and nouns describing difficult terms or words that you don't recognize. Regardless of whether you completely understand a word or not, replacing it with a synonym, either provided or one you more familiar with, may help you to understand what the questions are asking. Rather than wracking your mind about specific detailed information concerning a difficult term or word, try to use mental substitutes that are easier to understand.

The Trap of Familiarity

Don't just choose a word because you recognize it. On difficult questions, you may not recognize a number of words in the answer choices. The test writers don't put "make-believe" words on the test, so don't think that just because you only recognize all the words in one answer choice that that answer choice must be correct. If you only recognize words in one answer choice, then focus on that one. Is it correct? Try your best to determine if it is correct. If it is, that's great. If not, eliminate it. Each word and answer choice you eliminate increases your chances of getting the question correct, even if you then have to guess among the unfamiliar choices.

Eliminate Answers

Eliminate choices as soon as you realize they are wrong. But be careful! Make sure you consider all of the possible answer choices. Just because one appears right, doesn't mean that the next one won't be even better! The test writers will usually put more than one good answer choice for every question, so read all of them. Don't worry if you are stuck between two that seem right. By getting down to just two remaining possible choices, your odds are now 50/50. Rather than wasting too much time, play the odds. You are guessing, but guessing wisely because you've been able to knock out some of the answer choices that you know are wrong. If you are eliminating choices and realize that the last answer choice you are left with is also obviously wrong, don't panic. Start over and consider each choice again. There may easily be something that you missed the first time and will realize on the second pass.

Tough Questions

If you are stumped on a problem or it appears too hard or too difficult, don't waste time. Move on! Remember though, if you can quickly check for obviously incorrect answer choices, your chances of guessing correctly are greatly improved. Before you completely give up, at least try to knock out a couple of possible answers. Eliminate what you can and then guess at the remaining answer choices before moving on.

Brainstorm

If you get stuck on a difficult question, spend a few seconds quickly brainstorming. Run through the complete list of possible answer choices. Look at each choice and ask yourself, "Could this answer the question satisfactorily?" Go through each answer choice and consider it independently of the others. By systematically going through all possibilities, you may find something that you would otherwise overlook. Remember though that when you get stuck, it's important to try to keep moving.

Read Carefully

Understand the problem. Read the question and answer choices carefully. Don't miss the question because you misread the terms. You have plenty of time to read each question thoroughly and make sure you understand what is being asked. Yet a happy medium must be attained, so don't waste too much time. You must read carefully, but efficiently.

Face Value

When in doubt, use common sense. Always accept the situation in the problem at face value. Don't read too much into it. These problems will not require you to make huge leaps of logic. The test writers aren't trying to throw you off with a cheap trick. If you have to go beyond creativity and make a leap of logic in order to have an answer choice answer the question, then you should look at the other answer choices. Don't overcomplicate the problem by creating theoretical relationships or explanations that will warp time or space. These are normal problems rooted in reality. It's just that the applicable relationship or explanation may not be readily apparent and you have to figure things out. Use your common sense to interpret anything that isn't clear.

Prefixes

If you're having trouble with a word in the question or answer choices, try dissecting it. Take advantage of every clue that the word might include. Prefixes and suffixes can be a huge help. Usually they allow you to determine a basic meaning. Pre- means before, post- means after, pro - is positive, de- is negative. From these prefixes and suffixes, you can get an idea of the general meaning of the word and try to put it into context. Beware though of any traps. Just because con- is the opposite of pro-, doesn't necessarily mean congress is the opposite of progress!

Hedge Phrases

Watch out for critical hedge phrases, led off with words such as "likely," "may," "can," "sometimes," "often," "almost," "mostly," "usually," "generally," "rarely," and "sometimes." Question writers insert these hedge phrases to cover every possibility. Often an answer choice will be wrong simply because it leaves no room for exception. Unless the situation calls for them, avoid answer choices that have definitive words like "exactly," and "always."

Switchback Words

Stay alert for "switchbacks." These are the words and phrases frequently used to alert you to shifts in thought. The most common switchback word is "but." Others include "although," "however," "nevertheless," "on the other hand," "even though," "while," "in spite of," "despite," and "regardless of."

New Information

Correct answer choices will rarely have completely new information included. Answer choices typically are straightforward reflections of the material asked about and will directly relate to the question. If a new piece of information is included in an answer choice that doesn't even seem to relate to the topic being asked about, then that answer choice is likely incorrect. All of the information needed to answer the question is usually provided for you in the question. You should not have to make guesses that are unsupported or choose answer choices that require unknown information that cannot be reasoned from what is given.

Time Management

On technical questions, don't get lost on the technical terms. Don't spend too much time on any one question. If you don't know what a term means, then odds are you aren't going to get much further since you don't have a dictionary. You should be able to immediately recognize whether or not you know a term. If you don't, work with the other clues that you have—the other answer choices and terms provided—but don't waste too much time trying to figure out a difficult term that you don't know.

Contextual Clues

Look for contextual clues. An answer can be right but not the correct answer. The contextual clues will help you find the answer that is most right and is correct. Understand the context in which a phrase or statement is made. This will help you make important distinctions.

Don't Panic

Panicking will not answer any questions for you; therefore, it isn't helpful. When you first see the question, if your mind goes blank, take a deep breath. Force yourself to mechanically go through the steps of solving the problem using the strategies you've learned.

Pace Yourself

Don't get clock fever. It's easy to be overwhelmed when you're looking at a page full of questions, your mind is full of random thoughts and feeling confused, and the clock is ticking down faster than you would like. Calm down and maintain the pace that you have set for yourself. As long as you are on track by monitoring your pace, you are guaranteed to have enough time for yourself. When you get to the last few minutes of the test, it may seem like you won't have enough time left, but if you only have as many questions as you should have left at that point, then you're right on track!

Answer Selection

The best way to pick an answer choice is to eliminate all of those that are wrong, until only one is left and confirm that is the correct answer. Sometimes though, an answer choice may immediately look right. Be careful! Take a second to make sure that the other choices are not equally obvious. Don't make a hasty mistake. There are only two times that you should stop before checking other answers. First is when you are positive that the answer choice you have selected is correct. Second is when time is almost out and you have to make a quick guess!

Check Your Work

Since you will probably not know every term listed and the answer to every question, it is important that you get credit for the ones that you do know. Don't miss any questions through careless mistakes. If at all possible, try to take a second to look back over your answer selection and make sure you've selected the correct answer choice and haven't made a costly careless mistake (such as marking an answer choice that you didn't mean to mark). The time it takes for this quick double check should more than pay for itself in caught mistakes.

Beware of Directly Quoted Answers

Sometimes an answer choice will repeat word for word a portion of the question or reference section. However, beware of such exact duplication. It may be a trap! More than likely, the correct choice will paraphrase or summarize a point, rather than being exactly the same wording.

Slang

Scientific sounding answers are better than slang ones. An answer choice that begins "To compare the outcomes..." is much more likely to be correct than one that begins "Because some people insisted..."

Extreme Statements

Avoid wild answers that throw out highly controversial ideas that are proclaimed as established fact. An answer choice that states the "process should used in certain situations, if…" is much more likely to be correct than one that states the "process should be discontinued completely." The first is a calm rational statement and doesn't even make a definitive, uncompromising stance, using a hedge word "if" to provide wiggle room, whereas the second choice is a radical idea and far more extreme.

Answer Choice Families

When you have two or more answer choices that are direct opposites or parallels, one of them is usually the correct answer. For instance, if one answer choice states "x increases" and another answer choice states "x decreases" or "y increases," then those two or three answer choices are very similar in construction and fall into the same family of answer choices. A family of answer choices consists of two or three answer choices, very similar in construction, but often with directly opposite meanings. Usually the correct answer choice will be in that family of answer choices. The "odd man out" or answer choice that doesn't seem to fit the parallel construction of the other answer choices is more likely to be incorrect.

Special Report: How to Overcome Test Anxiety

The very nature of tests caters to some level of anxiety, nervousness, or tension, just as we feel for any important event that occurs in our lives. A little bit of anxiety or nervousness can be a good thing. It helps us with motivation, and makes achievement just that much sweeter. However, too much anxiety can be a problem, especially if it hinders our ability to function and perform.

"Test anxiety," is the term that refers to the emotional reactions that some test-takers experience when faced with a test or exam. Having a fear of testing and exams is based upon a rational fear, since the test-taker's performance can shape the course of an academic career. Nevertheless, experiencing excessive fear of examinations will only interfere with the test-taker's ability to perform and chance to be successful.

There are a large variety of causes that can contribute to the development and sensation of test anxiety. These include, but are not limited to, lack of preparation and worrying about issues surrounding the test.

Lack of Preparation

Lack of preparation can be identified by the following behaviors or situations:

Not scheduling enough time to study, and therefore cramming the night before the test or exam
Managing time poorly, to create the sensation that there is not enough time to do everything
Failing to organize the text information in advance, so that the study material consists of the entire text and not simply the pertinent information
Poor overall studying habits

Worrying, on the other hand, can be related to both the test taker, or many other factors around him/her that will be affected by the results of the test. These include worrying about:

Previous performances on similar exams, or exams in general
How friends and other students are achieving
The negative consequences that will result from a poor grade or failure

There are three primary elements to test anxiety. Physical components, which involve the same typical bodily reactions as those to acute anxiety (to be discussed below). Emotional factors have to do with fear or panic. Mental or cognitive issues concerning attention spans and memory abilities.

Physical Signals

There are many different symptoms of test anxiety, and these are not limited to mental and emotional strain. Frequently there are a range of physical signals that will let a test taker know that he/she is suffering from test anxiety. These bodily changes can include the following:

Perspiring
Sweaty palms
Wet, trembling hands
Nausea
Dry mouth
A knot in the stomach
Headache
Faintness
Muscle tension
Aching shoulders, back and neck
Rapid heart beat
Feeling too hot/cold

To recognize the sensation of test anxiety, a test-taker should monitor him/herself for the following sensations:

The physical distress symptoms as listed above
Emotional sensitivity, expressing emotional feelings such as the need to cry or laugh too much, or a sensation of anger or helplessness
A decreased ability to think, causing the test-taker to blank out or have racing thoughts that are hard to organize or control.

Though most students will feel some level of anxiety when faced with a test or exam, the majority can cope with that anxiety and maintain it at a manageable level. However, those who cannot are faced with a very real and very serious condition, which can and should be controlled for the immeasurable benefit of this sufferer.

Naturally, these sensations lead to negative results for the testing experience. The most common effects of test anxiety have to do with nervousness and mental blocking.

Nervousness

Nervousness can appear in several different levels:

The test-taker's difficulty, or even inability to read and understand the questions on the test

The difficulty or inability to organize thoughts to a coherent form

The difficulty or inability to recall key words and concepts relating to the testing questions (especially essays)

The receipt of poor grades on a test, though the test material was well known by the test taker

Conversely, a person may also experience mental blocking, which involves:

Blanking out on test questions

Only remembering the correct answers to the questions when the test has already finished.

Fortunately for test anxiety sufferers, beating these feelings, to a large degree, has to do with proper preparation. When a test taker has a feeling of preparedness, then anxiety will be dramatically lessened.

The first step to resolving anxiety issues is to distinguish which of the two types of anxiety are being suffered. If the anxiety is a direct result of a lack of preparation, this should be considered a normal reaction, and the anxiety level (as opposed to the test results) shouldn't be anything to worry about. However, if, when adequately prepared, the test-taker still panics, blanks out, or seems to overreact, this is not a fully rational reaction. While this can be considered normal too, there are many ways to combat and overcome these effects.

Remember that anxiety cannot be entirely eliminated, however, there are ways to minimize it, to make the anxiety easier to manage. Preparation is one of the best ways to minimize test anxiety. Therefore the following techniques are wise in order to best fight off any anxiety that may want to build.

To begin with, try to avoid cramming before a test, whenever it is possible. By trying to memorize an entire term's worth of information in one day, you'll be shocking your system, and not giving yourself a very good chance to absorb the information. This is an easy path to anxiety, so for those who suffer from test anxiety, cramming should not even be considered an option.

Instead of cramming, work throughout the semester to combine all of the material which is presented throughout the semester, and work on it gradually as the course goes by, making sure to master the main concepts first, leaving minor details for a week or so before the test.

To study for the upcoming exam, be sure to pose questions that may be on the examination, to gauge the ability to answer them by integrating the ideas from your texts, notes and lectures, as well as any supplementary readings.

If it is truly impossible to cover all of the information that was covered in that particular term, concentrate on the most important portions, that can be covered very well. Learn these concepts as best as possible, so that when the test comes, a goal can be made to use these concepts as presentations of your knowledge.

In addition to study habits, changes in attitude are critical to beating a struggle with test anxiety. In fact, an improvement of the perspective over the entire test-taking experience can actually help a test taker to enjoy studying and therefore improve the overall experience. Be certain not to overemphasize the significance of the grade - know that the result of the test is neither a reflection of self worth, nor is it a measure of intelligence; one grade will not predict a person's future success.

To improve an overall testing outlook, the following steps should be tried:

Keeping in mind that the most reasonable expectation for taking a test is to expect to try to demonstrate as much of what you know as you possibly can. Reminding ourselves that a test is only one test; this is not the only one, and there will be others.
The thought of thinking of oneself in an irrational, all-or-nothing term should be avoided at all costs.
A reward should be designated for after the test, so there's something to look forward to. Whether it be going to a movie, going out to eat, or simply visiting friends, schedule it in advance, and do it no matter what result is expected on the exam.

Test-takers should also keep in mind that the basics are some of the most important things, even beyond anti-anxiety techniques and studying. Never neglect the basic social, emotional and biological needs, in order to try to absorb information. In order to best achieve, these three factors must be held as just as important as the studying itself.

Study Steps

Remember the following important steps for studying:

Maintain healthy nutrition and exercise habits. Continue both your recreational activities and social pass times. These both contribute to your physical and emotional well being.
Be certain to get a good amount of sleep, especially the night before the test, because when you're overtired you are not able to perform to the best of your best ability.
Keep the studying pace to a moderate level by taking breaks when they are needed, and varying the work whenever possible, to keep the mind fresh instead of getting bored.
When enough studying has been done that all the material that can be learned has been learned, and the test taker is prepared for the test, stop studying and do

something relaxing such as listening to music, watching a movie, or taking a warm bubble bath.

There are also many other techniques to minimize the uneasiness or apprehension that is experienced along with test anxiety before, during, or even after the examination. In fact, there are a great deal of things that can be done to stop anxiety from interfering with lifestyle and performance. Again, remember that anxiety will not be eliminated entirely, and it shouldn't be. Otherwise that "up" feeling for exams would not exist, and most of us depend on that sensation to perform better than usual. However, this anxiety has to be at a level that is manageable.

Of course, as we have just discussed, being prepared for the exam is half the battle right away. Attending all classes, finding out what knowledge will be expected on the exam, and knowing the exam schedules are easy steps to lowering anxiety. Keeping up with work will remove the need to cram, and efficient study habits will eliminate wasted time. Studying should be done in an ideal location for concentration, so that it is simple to become interested in the material and give it complete attention. A method such as SQ3R (Survey, Question, Read, Recite, Review) is a wonderful key to follow to make sure that the study habits are as effective as possible, especially in the case of learning from a textbook. Flashcards are great techniques for memorization. Learning to take good notes will mean that notes will be full of useful information, so that less sifting will need to be done to seek out what is pertinent for studying. Reviewing notes after class and then again on occasion will keep the information fresh in the mind. From notes that have been taken summary sheets and outlines can be made for simpler reviewing.

A study group can also be a very motivational and helpful place to study, as there will be a sharing of ideas, all of the minds can work together, to make sure that everyone understands, and the studying will be made more interesting because it will be a social occasion.

Basically, though, as long as the test-taker remains organized and self confident, with efficient study habits, less time will need to be spent studying, and higher grades will be achieved.

To become self confident, there are many useful steps. The first of these is "self talk." It has been shown through extensive research, that self-talk for students who suffer from test anxiety, should be well monitored, in order to make sure that it contributes to self confidence as opposed to sinking the student. Frequently the self talk of test-anxious students is negative or self-defeating, thinking that everyone else is smarter and faster, that they always mess up, and that if they don't do well, they'll fail the entire course. It is important to decreasing anxiety that awareness is made of self talk. Try writing any negative self thoughts and then disputing them with a positive statement instead. Begin self-encouragement as though it was a friend speaking. Repeat positive statements to help reprogram the mind to believing in successes instead of failures.

Helpful Techniques

Other extremely helpful techniques include:

Self-visualization of doing well and reaching goals
While aiming for an "A" level of understanding, don't try to "overprotect" by setting your expectations lower. This will only convince the mind to stop studying in order to meet the lower expectations.
Don't make comparisons with the results or habits of other students. These are individual factors, and different things work for different people, causing different results.
Strive to become an expert in learning what works well, and what can be done in order to improve. Consider collecting this data in a journal.
Create rewards for after studying instead of doing things before studying that will only turn into avoidance behaviors.
Make a practice of relaxing - by using methods such as progressive relaxation, self-hypnosis, guided imagery, etc - in order to make relaxation an automatic sensation.
Work on creating a state of relaxed concentration so that concentrating will take on the focus of the mind, so that none will be wasted on worrying.
Take good care of the physical self by eating well and getting enough sleep.
Plan in time for exercise and stick to this plan.

Beyond these techniques, there are other methods to be used before, during and after the test that will help the test-taker perform well in addition to overcoming anxiety.

Before the exam comes the academic preparation. This involves establishing a study schedule and beginning at least one week before the actual date of the test. By doing this, the anxiety of not having enough time to study for the test will be automatically eliminated. Moreover, this will make the studying a much more effective experience, ensuring that the learning will be an easier process. This relieves much undue pressure on the test-taker.

Summary sheets, note cards, and flash cards with the main concepts and examples of these main concepts should be prepared in advance of the actual studying time. A topic should never be eliminated from this process. By omitting a topic because it isn't expected to be on the test is only setting up the test-taker for anxiety should it actually appear on the exam. Utilize the course syllabus for laying out the topics that should be studied. Carefully go over the notes that were made in class, paying special attention to any of the issues that the professor took special care to emphasize while lecturing in class. In the textbooks, use the chapter review, or if possible, the chapter tests, to begin your review.

It may even be possible to ask the instructor what information will be covered on the exam, or what the format of the exam will be (for example, multiple choice, essay, free form, true-false). Additionally, see if it is possible to find out how many questions will be on the test. If a review sheet or sample test has been offered by the professor, make good use of it, above anything else, for the preparation for the test. Another great resource for getting to know the examination is reviewing tests from previous semesters. Use these tests to review, and aim to achieve a 100% score on each of the possible topics. With a few exceptions, the goal that you set for yourself is the highest one that you will reach.

Take all of the questions that were assigned as homework, and rework them to any other possible course material. The more problems reworked, the more skill and confidence will form as a result. When forming the solution to a problem, write out each of the steps. Don't simply do head work. By doing as many steps on paper as possible, much clarification and therefore confidence will be formed. Do this with as many homework problems as possible, before checking the answers. By checking the answer after each problem, a reinforcement will exist, that will not be on the exam. Study situations should be as exam-like as possible, to prime the test-taker's system for the experience. By waiting to check the answers at the end, a psychological advantage will be formed, to decrease the stress factor.

Another fantastic reason for not cramming is the avoidance of confusion in concepts, especially when it comes to mathematics. 8-10 hours of study will become one hundred percent more effective if it is spread out over a week or at least several days, instead of doing it all in one sitting. Recognize that the human brain requires time in order to assimilate new material, so frequent breaks and a span of study time over several days will be much more beneficial.

Additionally, don't study right up until the point of the exam. Studying should stop a minimum of one hour before the exam begins. This allows the brain to rest and put things in their proper order. This will also provide the time to become as relaxed as possible when going into the examination room. The test-taker will also have time to eat well and eat sensibly. Know that the brain needs food as much as the rest of the body. With enough food and enough sleep, as well as a relaxed attitude, the body and the mind are primed for success.

Avoid any anxious classmates who are talking about the exam. These students only spread anxiety, and are not worth sharing the anxious sentimentalities.

Before the test also involves creating a positive attitude, so mental preparation should also be a point of concentration. There are many keys to creating a positive attitude. Should fears become rushing in, make a visualization of taking the exam, doing well, and seeing an A written on the paper. Write out a list of affirmations that will bring a feeling of confidence, such as "I am doing well in my English class," "I studied well and know my material," "I enjoy this class." Even if the affirmations aren't believed at first, it sends a positive message to the subconscious which will result in an alteration of the overall belief system, which is the system that creates reality.

If a sensation of panic begins, work with the fear and imagine the very worst! Work through the entire scenario of not passing the test, failing the entire course, and dropping out of school, followed by not getting a job, and pushing a shopping cart through the dark alley where you'll live. This will place things into perspective! Then, practice deep breathing and create a visualization of the opposite situation - achieving an "A" on the exam, passing the entire course, receiving the degree at a graduation ceremony.

On the day of the test, there are many things to be done to ensure the best results, as well as the most calm outlook. The following stages are suggested in order to maximize test-taking potential:

Begin the examination day with a moderate breakfast, and avoid any coffee or beverages with caffeine if the test taker is prone to jitters. Even people who are used to managing caffeine can feel jittery or light-headed when it is taken on a test day.
Attempt to do something that is relaxing before the examination begins. As last minute cramming clouds the mastering of overall concepts, it is better to use this time to create a calming outlook.
Be certain to arrive at the test location well in advance, in order to provide time to select a location that is away from doors, windows and other distractions, as well as giving enough time to relax before the test begins.
Keep away from anxiety generating classmates who will upset the sensation of stability and relaxation that is being attempted before the exam.
Should the waiting period before the exam begins cause anxiety, create a self-distraction by reading a light magazine or something else that is relaxing and simple.

During the exam itself, read the entire exam from beginning to end, and find out how much time should be allotted to each individual problem. Once writing the exam, should more time be taken for a problem, it should be abandoned, in order to begin another problem. If there is time at the end, the unfinished problem can always be returned to and completed.

Read the instructions very carefully - twice - so that unpleasant surprises won't follow during or after the exam has ended.

When writing the exam, pretend that the situation is actually simply the completion of homework within a library, or at home. This will assist in forming a relaxed atmosphere, and will allow the brain extra focus for the complex thinking function.

Begin the exam with all of the questions with which the most confidence is felt. This will build the confidence level regarding the entire exam and will begin a quality momentum. This will also create encouragement for trying the problems where uncertainty resides.

Going with the "gut instinct" is always the way to go when solving a problem. Second guessing should be avoided at all costs. Have confidence in the ability to do well.

For essay questions, create an outline in advance that will keep the mind organized and make certain that all of the points are remembered. For multiple choice, read every answer, even if the correct one has been spotted - a better one may exist.

Continue at a pace that is reasonable and not rushed, in order to be able to work carefully. Provide enough time to go over the answers at the end, to check for small errors that can be corrected.

Should a feeling of panic begin, breathe deeply, and think of the feeling of the body releasing sand through its pores. Visualize a calm, peaceful place, and include all of the sights, sounds and sensations of this image. Continue the deep breathing, and take a few minutes to continue this with closed eyes. When all is well again, return to the test.

If a "blanking" occurs for a certain question, skip it and move on to the next question. There will be time to return to the other question later. Get everything done that can be done, first, to guarantee all the grades that can be compiled, and to build all of the confidence possible. Then return to the weaker questions to build the marks from there.

Remember, one's own reality can be created, so as long as the belief is there, success will follow. And remember: anxiety can happen later, right now, there's an exam to be written!

After the examination is complete, whether there is a feeling for a good grade or a bad grade, don't dwell on the exam, and be certain to follow through on the reward that was promised...and enjoy it! Don't dwell on any mistakes that have been made, as there is nothing that can be done at this point anyway.

Additionally, don't begin to study for the next test right away. Do something relaxing for a while, and let the mind relax and prepare itself to begin absorbing information again.

From the results of the exam - both the grade and the entire experience, be certain to learn from what has gone on. Perfect studying habits and work some more on confidence in order to make the next examination experience even better than the last one.

Learn to avoid places where openings occurred for laziness, procrastination and day dreaming.

Use the time between this exam and the next one to better learn to relax, even learning to relax on cue, so that any anxiety can be controlled during the next exam. Learn how to relax the body. Slouch in your chair if that helps. Tighten and then relax all of the different muscle groups, one group at a time, beginning with the feet and then working all the way up to the neck and face. This will ultimately relax the muscles more than they were to begin with. Learn how to breathe deeply and comfortably, and focus on this breathing going in and out as a relaxing thought. With every exhale, repeat the word "relax."

As common as test anxiety is, it is very possible to overcome it. Make yourself one of the test-takers who overcome this frustrating hindrance.

Additional Bonus Material

Due to our efforts to try to keep this book to a manageable length, we've created a link that will give you access to all of your additional bonus material.

Please visit http://www.mometrix.com/bonus948/clepamerlit to access the information.